DEBUNK

Arm Yourself With the
Tenets of Critical Thinking

Plus: How to Combat
DISinformation and
FAKE News

DEBUNK

Arm Yourself With the
Tenets of Critical Thinking

Plus: How to Combat
DISinformation and
FAKE News

Sam McCollough

TENET PUBLICATIONS
FLORIDA

TENET PUBLICATIONS
Florida

An Imprint of Simple Virtues, LLC
201 N US HIGHWAY 1 STE D10 #1117
Jupiter, FL 33477
United States

TENET PUBLICATIONS and the distinctive Tenet Publications logo are trademarks of Simple Virtues, LLC.

Copyright © 2024 by Sam McCollough. All rights reserved.

ISBN 979-8-9915610-1-3

Library of Congress Control Number: 2024919604

For information about custom editions and premium or corporate purchases, contact marketing@tenetpublications.com

Thinking Man by J4P4N on openclipart.org

www.tenetpublications.com

Acknowledgements

I would like to thank my editors, Danielle Matthews and Jim Jacklich, for helping me make this book more readable and more correct. Jim is no longer with us, but his help as an editor/philosopher was invaluable to me in the early stages of writing this book. Any remaining errors are, of course, mine.

I am grateful to my family for their support and in particular to my children for reminding me every day why it is important that we leave them and future generations a world where reason and truth matter.

I dedicate this book to the millions of people who are being taken in by charlatans, who are being lied to every day in an ongoing, deliberate, malevolent way, being purposely misled into acting against their own self-interests. I hope the tools herein can help you to see through the onslaught of deception so you can make decisions for yourself and your loved ones that are truly in alignment with what you would want.

September 2024
Jupiter, Florida

TABLE OF CONTENTS

Acknowledgements vii

Introduction 1

Critical Thinking 9

Principles of Logic and Logical Fallacies 19

Types of Causes and Effects 23

Axioms of Science 29

The Scientific Method 35

Good Current Science, Outdated Science, and Pseudoscience 51

Conspiracy Theories 57

Epistemology 67

Agnotology 73

Debunking Misinformation, Disinformation, Fake News, and Deep Fakes 81

Conclusions & Recap 91

Tenets of Critical Thinking 95

For Further Reading 101

Appendix: Logical Fallacies 105

Glossary 123

Index 129

Introduction

The Information Age is said to have come in three phases, each one represented by new technologies that enhanced what came before:

Phase 1 – Newspapers, radio, and television

Phase 2 – The Internet, satellites, computers and mobile phones

Phase 3 – Social and digital/new media

Now we have transitioned into a new age, defined by Interned-enabled devices, the Age of IoT (Internet of Things), which it is predicted will become the Age of Surveillance because the powers that be can use these devices to track our movements.[1]

The invention and widespread use of computers, and especially the proliferation of the Internet, brought us into a time when ordinary people have immediate access to more information than professors, librarians, and heads of state had access to only a short time ago. This is quite a paradigm shift in only a few generations. It is empowering, but it is also dangerous—the

---

[1] 2020: END OF THE INFORMATION AGE AND BEGINNING OF THE AGE OF IOT, Boundless Digital Media, Nov. 1, 2020. Retrieved from https://medium.com/@boundless_ke/2020-end-of-the-information-age-and-beginning-of-the-age-of-iot-67023adcc348 Aug. 19, 2024

Information Age is also the Misinformation and Disinformation Age, and it is easier to find bad information on the Internet, especially with the addition of AI, than good. Add to that all of the entities that have been popping up seemingly with the express purpose of disseminating fake news, and the recent invention of deep fakes that are becoming harder and harder to detect, and the need for *critical thinking*, which provides you with a toolkit for spotting bunk, becomes more and more vital. Tenet: Many vested interests can benefit from disseminating bad information (usually by making money off us or by keeping themselves in power). Also, those seeking profit or power will often control what information is released to us and manipulate the information or its interpretation. Consider the actions of the sugar industry in skewing research to make its members' products seem safer and making fats look more dangerous, thereby impacting consumers' eating habits for decades.[2]

---

[2] O'Connor, Anahad (2016, September 12). How the Sugar Industry Shifted Blame to Fat, *New York Times.* Retrieved from http://mobile.nytimes.com/2016/09/13/well/eat/how-the-sugar-industry-shifted-blame-to-fat.html?mwrsm=Facebook&_r=0&referer=http://lm.facebook.com/lsr.php?u=http://www.nytimes.com/2016/09/13/well/eat/how-the-sugar-industry-shifted-blame-to-fat.html?mwrsm=Facebook&ext=1473776951&hash=AcnD1Gmh43qik8NG8IpomricV1Bx77NqbkMTv1Iu6rBJ_w&_rdr

There is so much information available on the Internet today that it's tempting to bypass the reading of books, thinking that whatever you need to know, you can just Google it. The danger is the amount of misinformation and disinformation not easily distinguishable from what is accurate and true. Also, the nature of the algorithms designed to keep us engaged on social media, clickbait, and our fading attention spans have conspired to train us to consume limited information quickly instead of taking the time to read at length. However, I would argue that it is necessary. There is a very real tangential value of reading where you not only learn from the contents of the books that you read, that foundation of knowledge also helps immensely to enable you to identify good and bad information online and elsewhere. The great value of learning from professional teachers and professors is that the information presented has been curated and validated for you, so you can have a higher level of confidence in its validity and relevance than if you went searching for it on your own. Similarly, even if you do not have the means to acquire or access to formalized school, you can become self-taught, but, again, this should be from consuming more in-depth material, not the reading or skimming of online articles. In this way, you learn to evaluate and judge for yourself the likely validity of information you find online and elsewhere.

Also consider, it is thought by many researchers that our brains did not evolve to reason well, but to socialize well. There are many times when our confirmation bias works not just to confirm our own biases, but those of our tribe—if coming to a wrong conclusion or holding an incorrect opinion helps us to fit in well with our tribe, even though it is incorrect, that can still benefit us and confer survival advantage.[3] This is why, even if you are intelligent, you still need to train yourself to analyze information in a way that helps you to avoid the pitfalls of confirmation bias and other cognitive mistakes that we all make on a regular basis.

For Further Reading is a good place to start for suggestions about some good books to start with.

I'll also take this opportunity to put in a plug for libraries. You do not need to buy the books in *For Further Reading*; just ask your local library to get one for you and check it out for free!

As an example of misinformation, I was looking for some information about the Big Bang and Inflation

---

[3] The Social Brain: Neural Basis of Social Knowledge, Ralph Adolphs, published in final edited form as:
Annu Rev Psychol. 2009; 60: 693–716, Retrieved from
https://www.ncbi.nlm.nih.gov/pmc/articles/PMC2588649/# September 4, 2024

Theory recently while making some edits to another book I am working on about the Universe, cosmology, and physics. The article stated that the Universe started with a point singularity at the Big Bang. Well, that sounds right, and many people would say it is right, but because of more in-depth study I was able to recognize that this is outdated thinking, so I continued my search for a more up-to-date article.

With the advent of AI (Artificial Intelligence) and the frighteningly realistic images, audio, and even video it can be used to produce (note that I didn't say "it can produce"—AI doesn't create anything, *people* use AI to create things—and those people can have their own agendas, sometimes malicious), critical thinking skills are more important than ever. It is harder to distinguish real from fake and truth from lies. At the time of this writing, there is usually something you can spot in an AI generated image, e.g., too many hands, that give it away. But AI apps will only become smarter, and it will become more difficult to spot fakes. See the *Debunking* chapter for resources to help defend against misinformation, disinformation, fake news, and deep fakes. Always remember, though: maybe the biggest reason why it is important to hone your critical thinking skills, even though these debunking resources exist, is that the volume and speed at which all the bunk is coming at us will only continue to increase. It is impossible to keep up and take the time to look it all up! You need a trained mind that can dismiss most of the bunk out of hand, without having to take the time to check it out.

Tenet: Being able to question and analyze information is the most important skill that anyone can have now, and we should teach ourselves and our children the tools for this. It is helpful to first provide a foundation of basics that have been hard-earned over the centuries and then to use that understanding to tear down the edifice of bad knowledge (unlearn the wrong things).

To that end, we will first discuss critical thinking in general, and then we will look at some areas of critical thinking that deserve special attention:

- Principles of logic and logical fallacies
- Types of causes and effects
- Axioms of science
- The Scientific Method
- Differentiating between good current science, outdated science, and pseudoscience
- Conspiracy theories
- Epistemology

- Agnotology (the nature of misinformation)
- Debunking, fake news, and deep fakes

I will note *Tenets* within the text in each chapter and provide a list of all the tenets at the end of the book, as I think it useful to have a readily accessed list of central points to refer to.

Critical Thinking

A toolbox for analyzing and evaluating the accuracy of relevant information.

Critical thinking is about evaluating information that you receive, no matter the medium (e.g., the newspaper or a news program, a book, social media, etc.) or the method of perception (e.g., if you heard it, read it, or even if you saw it for yourself). Instead of just accepting it as true; be skeptical. It is also important to express your own opinions clearly and adequately so that others can fairly and accurately evaluate what *you* say.

Be skeptical. Don't believe everything you read, see, hear, or perceive by any of your other senses, either. Don't believe everything you're told, even if you are told by a person or by many people in positions of authority, even if you are told many times over your whole life, and even if everyone else seems to believe it or even to know that it is true.

For example, there exists a meme of knowledge that it is easier to stand an egg on its end on the vernal (spring) equinox. This is a perfect example of people just believing what they hear without subjecting it to *critical thinking*. The first questions that should be asked are "*Why* would this be so? What conceivable *mechanism* would cause this phenomenon?" One possible mechanism does come to mind: Maybe the fact that the Earth is tilted to point more directly at the Sun, so the gravitational pull of the Sun is helping the egg to stand up. This does sound at least *conceivable*, but does that mean it is plausible? Is the gravitational pull on one part of an egg really going to be significantly stronger than on another? Wouldn't it also matter where we live? It would seem that the date of the equinox would only favor egg-standing for those at the equator. And why would it just be the vernal equinox? Why wouldn't it work just as well on the autumnal equinox, when the equator also is pointing directly at the sun?

  Fortunately, we don't need to simply debate the relevant questions. We can resolve the issue by observation, hypothesis, and experiment. Tenet: As expressed by Francis Bacon in his "Novum Organum" in 1620, "Whether or no (sic) anything can be known, can be settled not by arguing, but by trying." Francis Bacon wasn't the first person to test things experimentally (Alhazen and other Arab scientists did so during the Golden Age of Islam), but he does get credit for writing down how to do it. He is credited with inventing the Scientific Method with his publication of Novum Organum in 1620 in which he laid out the three fundamental pillars of the scientific method: observation, hypothesis and experiment.[4]

In other words, we can test it ourselves and see if it "holds up" (i.e., is confirmed or verified). Fortunately, this has been done by others, but feel free to test it out for yourself, too. It's a nice example of a scientific experiment that anyone can conduct.

Let's say someone waited until the vernal equinox and tried to stand an egg on its end and found that after a few tries, they could indeed do it. This would seem to support the hypothesis. Or would it? There is a very common concept in science called the "control group." What this means in this case is that we must also try standing eggs on end on days other than the vernal equinox. Remember, the hypothesis is that it is *easier* on this one day than on other days.
This has been tested, and it turns out that it is just as easy to stand eggs on end on any random day of the year.[5] So remember: Don't believe everything you hear

---

[4] Hart-Davis et al, *The Science Book, Big Ideas Simply Explained* (DK | Penguin Random House, 2015), 45.
[5] Mikkelson, David (1999, March 17). Egg Balancing on the Equinox, Snopes. Retrieved from http://www.snopes.com/science/equinox.asp

(be skeptical). Use critical thinking, research and experimentation. Tenet

Tenet: In critical thinking, the focus is on *how to* think, not *what to* think, on the tools for analyzing information and identifying that which is likely to be true and that which is likely to be false, as well as that which should be questioned and perhaps for which judgment should not yet be rendered.

Numerous studies show that our reasoning abilities are suspect. Worse than that, they seem to be designed not to help us to make sound decisions, but to confirm our own existing positions and those of the groups with which we identify. Once we form an opinion or join a group that is organized around opinions, we then accept only new information that confirms those opinions and reject any that challenges them. This is commonly called *confirmation bias*, and we usually assume that the confirmation that it refers to is confirmation of our own opinions, but it also has been called *my side bias*, highlighting that it also, or perhaps mostly, actually refers to confirmation of the opinions of our tribe (our "tribe," can be any group that we identify with and/or belong to, from our immediate family to our political party, our nation, our race, our religion, etcetera). In her article *Why Facts Don't*

Change Our Minds, Elizabeth Colbert discusses the main points of numerous studies since the 1970s that seek to understand the ways in which our reasoning abilities seem so faulty and to explain why this is so.[6]

Here are the cognitive flaws highlighted in these studies:

1. We form opinions based on insufficient information, often confusing correlation with causation.
2. Once we form an opinion, we tend to keep it, even when presented with compelling evidence to the contrary.
3. We are much better at spotting the weaknesses in the arguments of others than we are at seeing them in our own arguments or those of our own tribes.

A landmark study cited in the article showed how we are not reliably reasonable in our ability to change our minds in the face of new information or to recognize when we might not have enough information to even form an opinion. An important question discussed in the article is *why is this so*? If we are *Homo sapiens*,

---

[6] *Why Facts Don't Change Our Minds, New discoveries about the human mind show the limitations of reason*, Elizabeth Kolbert, The New Yorker, 2/27/2017. Accessed 3/21/2018 from https://www.newyorker.com/magazine/2017/02/27/why-facts-dont-change-our-minds.

which means "thinking man," and our ability to reason is what separates us from the rest of the animal kingdom, you'd think we'd be better at it. After all, you would assume that the ability to reason evolved because it confers a survival advantage. If our reasoning is so bad, why did natural selection allow it to evolve?

The authors of a book reviewed in the article, *The Enigma of Reason*, say that we evolved reason not so much for problem solving in the conventional sense, but for solving the problem of how to live in social groups. If being a successfully integrated member of a tribe confers more survival advantage than being factually correct does, then it is easy to see how this could be so.

However, I'd like to point out what is perhaps a key distinction to be made between different types and purposes of reasoning that may also help to explain why both types of survival advantage could be served simultaneously by the evolution of our reason:

Types of reasoning:
1. Identifying immediate needs and threats and how to address them.
2. Forming opinions about big-picture questions, such as public welfare, gun control, etc.

Purposes of reasoning:
1. To accomplish a task, such as hunting prey, building a shelter, etc.
2. To form or reinforce group identity.

In both cases, Number 1 is associated with short-term survival, and Number 2 with socialization. Socialization is, of course, important to long-term survival—we need to form groups with whom to address immediate threats, hunt, build, etc. However, if we happen to find ourselves in a threatening situation that requires immediate action to survive, or presented with a task such as making a shelter, and the other person that we are with has widely-different political views than our own, we will most likely still opt to work together to address the immediate threat or accomplish the immediate task. The reasoning skills that we employ to do so will be more task-driven and mechanical in nature (such as how to use available tools to do what needs doing) rather than forming big-picture opinions about long-term policy. In modern times, most of us put aside our political differences at our jobs and work together to get the job done. It points to the differences in the kinds of reasoning involved in these two contexts that we usually can't even figure out the political leanings of our coworkers just by working with them on a task.

It seems to me that the questions asked were only designed to test the second type of reasoning, and perhaps we aren't as helpless at the first kind of reasoning. It also seems plausible that we could have evolved our reasoning originally to accomplish the first type, but then naturally tried to apply it to the second type. Also, the reason why we are so bad at the second type could be simply because of the much greater complexity of the problems that the second type seeks to solve. It is far easier to solve the problems of (and to agree on the solution for) making a spear or changing a flat tire than differentiating between real and fake suicide notes (or forming an opinion about how good we are at doing so).

We have access to many tools for improving our critical thinking. Second only to the ability to read, "... no other skill is more important than our ability to reason. Yet, strangely, no required course dedicated to reasoning skills exists as a part of our regular school curriculum...."[7] Tenet: A proper education includes being equipped with critical thinking skills, and it is the

---

[7] Brandon Royal, The Little Blue Thinking Book – 50 Powerful Principles for Clear and Effective Thinking (Fall River Press, 2010), 6.

duty of all parents (or guardians or caregivers) to do their best to ensure that their kids have a proper education, and to themselves provide the aspects of a necessary education that their children's schools fail to provide. To that end, it is therefore also necessary that parents educate themselves to be able to ensure their children's education.

Principles of Logic and Logical Fallacies

All logical statements and arguments follow a structure, whether the person making the claim realizes it or not. Because of this, all claims can be analyzed to see if they adhere to logic or if they commit one or more logical fallacies (errors). Tenet: Note that we can and should use these analytical tools not just with the statements of others, but our own, as well. This is important because we all filter information through our own *Confirmation Bias*, which means that we are more likely to believe information that supports what we already think or want to think than information that contradicts it.

Tenet: A logical argument always follows some version of the structure:

Assumption(s) + Evidence = Conclusion

For the conclusion to be valid, the following must all hold up to scrutiny:

1. The *assumption(s)* must be valid.
2. The *evidence* must be supported as factual.

3. The logical premise connecting the assumptions and the evidence to the conclusion must be valid.

So, when arguing against a claim, you are attacking one or more of these three aspects of the claim.

Assumptions are a good place to start. Common errors made with assumptions include:

- Stating two (or more) things as equivalent when they are not (or are not in this situation)
- Stating that one thing caused another when it did not (or when the correlation is low, coincidental, or maybe even reversed—e.g., a didn't cause b; b caused a).

The evidence might also be questionable. Is the evidence claimed true in all situations and at all times?

The logic connecting the assumptions and the evidence to the conclusion might be fallacious. Common arguments include:

- Since a is a member of group b, and all members of group b are cs, then a is a c.

- Since *a* is a *b*, and *b*s always do [activity] *c*, *a* must/would do / has done [activity] *c*.
- and the converse of this: Since *a* is a *b*, and *b*s never do [activity] *c*, *a* has not/would not/will not do [activity] *c*.

Example:

Since Congressman *a* is a Republican (evidence), and Republicans are hawks (assumption 1) that will always vote in favor of going to war (assumption 2), we know that Congressman *a* will vote in favor of going to war in *Anyland* (conclusion).

In this argument, we can easily evaluate the evidence that Congressman *a* is a Republican and verify that it is true. The assumptions that Republicans are all hawks and that hawks will vote in favor of any war are both questionable. Both assumptions are guilty of the Hasty Generalization logical fallacy.

The logical fallacies that occur when making the above kinds of statements usually fit one of several common types of logical fallacy. See Appendix A for a listing of types of logical fallacies and examples.

Types of Causes and Effects

A common dictum that cautions against assuming that one thing caused another just because it preceded it is that *correlation does not imply causation*. This is also known as the *post-hoc, ergo propter-hoc* (after this, therefore because of this) logical fallacy. In other words, just because two or more events coincided in space and time doesn't mean that one caused the other. Note that I said the two events *coincided* in space and time. That's why we call it a *coincidence* when this happens without a cause-and-effect link between the events.

For a cause-and-effect link to exist between events, these three things must be true:

- There must be temporal precedence—the cause must occur before the effect. If inflation hits a nation, and then that nation goes to war, you can't say that the war caused the inflation.
- There must also be a logical connection—the events must be related to each other. If I close a door and then the phone rings, it's likely that me closing the door didn't cause the phone to ring. That's an obvious example of unrelated events, but there are times when it is less obvious. This

is a good place to talk about magical thinking. There are people who think that if you, for example, say that your team is going to win the game, you've "jinxed" it, and your team either will now lose or is now more likely to lose. Wouldn't it be wonderful to have that kind of power, that kind of control over the course of events! A belief in jinxes and the like implies I can sway the outcome of future events by what I say, even if there is no logical connection between what I say and the future events.

- Finally, the logical connection between the events must be *direct*—that is, it can't be just a coincidence that one event followed another. If my car stalls just as it runs out of gas, that is a direct relationship, but just because my car stalls doesn't *necessarily* mean that I ran out of gas—the timing chain or belt could have slipped or broken, for example, or another cause that I may not even be aware of. This suggests an important point about recognizing and accepting uncertainty and our limitations of knowledge: be careful about thinking you know all the possibilities—there will be times when it is tempting to think, "yes, this must be the case" because you can't think of any other possibility. Remember that no one can be an expert in everything, and there may be possibilities that haven't occurred to you (even if you are an expert, actually).

So, once two or more events are indeed related causally, think about what *type* of cause the cause is. If we say that in a mechanistic Universe, every observed effect has a natural cause, then it will help us to understand a little about what kinds of causes (logically) there are:

- Sufficient cause: This is the only cause required to produce the effect (However, it might not be *necessary* (i.e., another cause or other causes could be sufficient to produce the effect)
    - Example: Walking is sufficient to cause your body to move from one place to another. However, it is not *necessary*—your body could be moved from one place to another by a car, for example.
- Necessary cause: This cause is necessary to produce the effect, but it may not be sufficient (i.e., another cause or other causes may also be required).
    - Example: Adding gas to your car is necessary to use it to move the car from

one place to another, but it may not be sufficient if your car has a mechanical issue preventing it from working.
- Component cause*:* A cause that contributes to the effect. It may or not be necessary and it is never sufficient by itself.
  - Examples: The gas in the car example is a necessary component cause; the car having an automatic transmission may or may not be necessary (it depends on the knowledge of the driver).

There are also multiple types of relationships between causes and effects:
- Single cause, multiple effect: One action or event produces more than one result.
- Multiple cause, single effect: This is the opposite, or converse, of single cause, multiple effect, where you have more than one action or event producing no more than one result.
- Causal chain (domino effect): In this situation, one or more actions or events produce one or more effects, and in the case of at least one of those effects, another effect occurs, and each subsequent effect becomes the cause for yet

another effect, unless interrupted at any point, at which point the chain is disrupted.
- Multiple cause, multiple effect: More than one action or event produces more than one result.[8][9]

Identifying these ways of looking at things helps us analyze our own thinking. It is very useful in medicine to determine what conditions lead to transmission of disease, and it can also be useful in our everyday lives.

---

[8] *Cause and Effect*, Owen Williams, University of Pennsylvania School of Arts and Sciences. Accessed 8/14/2024 from https://www.english.upenn.edu/graduate/resources/teachweb/owcause.html.
[9] *Cause and Effect | Definition, Relationship & Examples*, Jeremy Cook, Study.com. Accessed 8/14/2024 from https://study.com/academy/lesson/cause-and-effect-relationship-definition-examples-quiz.html.

Axioms of Science

Tenet: As discussed in the previous chapter, logic is a necessary component of critical thinking, but it is not always sufficient. Some knowledge cannot be deduced from argument alone; we must test our theories and see if they hold up to scientific scrutiny. The scientific method is more reliable than the use of pure reason to arrive at what is true. To do this, we must have a foundation to start from.

First, let's define the term *axiom*. To say that something is *axiomatic* is to say that is has been well-established as factual, is accepted as such, and/or is self-evidently true.

Tenet: There are basic assumptions (axioms) in science that are accepted universally:[10]

1. There are natural causes for events. A few corollaries can be deduced and are important to state, since the temptations to break them are so common:

    A. If you can't identify a natural cause for an event, that doesn't mean that one doesn't

---

[10] Basic assumptions of science. The University of California, Berkeley (2017). Retrieved from http://undsci.berkeley.edu/article/basic_assumptions

exist. It may be just that you didn't know where to look or because one hasn't been found yet (and perhaps will be in the future).

B. If you can't identify a natural cause for an event, that doesn't imply the necessity of a magical entity (e.g., a deity) to cause it (see A).

2. Naturalistic evidence should be used to explain those events.
3. Cause and effect relationships in the world operate consistently and predictably.

An example of what it means to say that these are axiomatic is that, if you conduct an experiment more than once and you get differing results, that doesn't mean that #3 is incorrect, it means that there was a difference in how the experiments were conducted.

4. The laws of nature operate consistently throughout the Universe.
5. Knowledge is advanced not through intuition or argument, but rather by empirical observation and experiment.

Now, regarding number five, this does not mean that *seeds of knowledge* cannot be generated via intuition or logic. They can be and are all the time. However, to *validate the intuition*, observation and experiment are necessary.

When there is something that we cannot explain (with current knowledge and technology), that is not evidence in favor of a divine explanation. That is a logical fallacy called a non-sequitur, which means that one proposition does not follow from another. An equivalent non-sequitur analysis is to say that because the cavemen cannot explain why it rained, it must be because of the rain dance that was performed by a shaman at last night's ceremony. This is also called a *post-hoc, ergo propter-hoc* fallacy, meaning that just because b followed a doesn't imply that a caused b. This fallacy is also cautioned against by the common dictum which states that *correlation does not imply causation.* Tenet In this case, this means that just because two events are correlated in time (and/or space) does not imply that one caused the other. Note that it is advances in knowledge and technology that enable us to answer a question (why it rains) that was once beyond our abilities and therefore left to superstitions to answer. The same can be said as to the question of why our Universe exists—because we don't currently possess the knowledge and technology to answer this question in a naturalistic way, many people defer to an answer based on superstition, that God did it. Note that the idea of God making it rain galaxies is not that different from the shaman making it rain in the previous example. We now know that every raindrop contains more atoms than there are stars in any galaxy, as well as many living organisms, making each raindrop a veritable world of its own (so the shaman wouldn't be simply creating drops of water, but complex microcosms—quite an impressive feat).

It is a valid question to ask why and how, if we accept these axioms at face value, without evidence for them, they are any different from religious dogmas? Here is the answer: Axioms define assumptions that are made to frame questions (e.g., if x is true, why does y happen?), whereas dogmas merely state that x is true. Axioms of science are assumed in order to answer questions about the natural world.
Another way to think of it is:
> Axioms are of the form 'Assume <some statement> is true'. Dogmas are of the form '<some statement> is true'.

Dogmas need to be believed, whereas axioms of science are assumed in order to do science. It's kind of like defining the rules of a game.[11] If you want to play the science game, follow these rules or the game doesn't work. If you don't want to play the science game, that's fine—play your game instead. If you want to play the supernatural game, then you can play by those rules. To the fact that you will still get to benefit from the fruits of the efforts of those of us who play the science game,* I can only say, to quote *Maui* from the movie *Moana*, "You're welcome!"

*An *extremely* abbreviated list of those fruits includes:

1. Modern medicine, the germ theory of disease, and the many, many cures, inoculations, and treatments that have come from it.
2. Modern technology, including air travel, all forms of computers, cell phones, all of the other modern conveniences that make our lives so much easier and better than ever before in human history, and all medical technology that supports item 1.
3. All of the fascinating knowledge about the physical world, including the Universe, galaxies, our Solar System, the Sun and other planets and

---

[11] What is the difference between dogma and an axiom?, *Philosophy*, various contributors and dates, retrieved from https://philosophy.stackexchange.com/questions/5922/what-is-the-difference-between-dogma-and-an-axiom September 4, 2024.

their moons, and all of the elements and subatomic particles and fundamental building blocks of nature and their workings, all of which supports items 1 and 2.

You're welcome.

The Scientific Method

We have been discussing critical thinking and skepticism. Both are necessary components of science, but they are not sufficient. People speak of the cold study of science, but that doesn't do it justice. Science starts with wonder, creativity, and intuition. That's where hypotheses come from. What separates science from other human enterprises that include wonder, creativity, and intuition is that it then subjects these hypotheses to testing and observation and tries to prove them wrong.

    The scientific method is the most reliable method of discovering how natural phenomena work. Tenet There are areas of life that aren't subject to being proven or disproven by the scientific method, but these become fewer over time as technology advances. The scientific method is not perfect and is subject to errors resulting from human fallibility, but the processes of public publishing and peer review help to give the scientific enterprise self-correcting mechanisms that no other method of gaining knowledge has ever before had in the history of human inquiry. Even the social sciences have embraced evidence-based practice to employ principles of the scientific method to affect the greatest good. In these ways and others, morally-sound ethics can be derived from science. Tenet

Let us define a few terms. People often get hung up on just what is meant by "science" as a noun and prefer to speak of "the scientific method." However, they are different.

The Scientific Method is a process that includes:
- Making an observation about a natural phenomenon
- Making a guess as to the cause of the observed phenomenon
- Devising a test to see if this guess is accurate
- Conducting and repeating the test
- Documenting the results
- Sharing the results with others so that they can try to either reproduce or contradict your results.

To simplify, the scientific method is a process for observing, predicting, and testing natural phenomena. Here is a mnemonic device to help remember it: I "choose" to use the scientific method. Another word for "choose" is "opt." I opt for the scientific method.

OPT = Observe, Predict, Test.

Three simple steps

1. Observe something

2. Make a **P**rediction as to either:

    A. The cause of what you observed, or

    B. What will happen if you try to cause a change to it

3. **T**est it.

Tenet: We all do science all the time, mostly without realizing it, and here are two common examples to convince you.

One example that is at once the simplest and the most complex, the most ancient and the most modern, the most personal and the most universal, is what we do when seeing someone who is sick:

1. We **O**bserve the symptoms.
2. We **P**redict the cause(s) of the symptoms and what the result of a treatment (e.g., giving a medication) would be.
3. We **T**est the prediction by giving the medication.

After observing the results, we either confirm that our prediction was right and continue the same treatment or, if we were wrong, we may make another prediction and conduct another test (treatment or medication).

Another universal and even more common example of science in practice is experimentation with cooking. The "observation" in this case is that we want a certain outcome (kind of meal, flavor combination, etc.) The prediction is that if we use these ingredients and prepare them in this way, we will get the desired result. We test it by preparing the meal (following the recipe), and then tasting the outcome. If we confirm our prediction, we might save that recipe to use again. If it turns out badly, the experiment failed, and we might try another experiment next time.

There are also professionals that conduct experiments for the above two examples, and we value their opinions and follow their recipes or their treatment recommendations when we or our loved ones get sick or when we are planning meals. Both practices (cooking and treating the sick), however, are quite complex (the latter far more than the former), and even professionals can get things wrong.

Why, if science often gets things wrong, do I still say it is the best way we have of finding knowledge about the natural world?
"Science" refers to the worldwide professional and academic scientific enterprise that investigates the natural world using the scientific method, research protocols, publication and peer review to increase our understanding and solve problems.

What do we mean by "the natural world?" Many resources define it as *excluding* what is created or caused by human activity,[12] but I think that muddies the waters and propagates the myth that we (humans) are separate from nature, that we are not animals. The branches of science that study us include chemistry, biology and medicine, which also apply to other animals, so how exactly would you separate human chemistry from "animal" chemistry? Likewise, the study of biology is the study of *all* life, and medicine certainly applies equally to other animals as well as to us. The natural world also includes the non-living world, of course, such as Earth and all structures, objects, and phenomena on it, including land and sea, mountains, deserts, forests and the atmosphere; and all of the processes that cause all of these to interact with each other, such as plate tectonics and volcanism, weather and erosion, solar effects, and also the effects of the living world on the non-living world, the biological processes such as animals changing their environment. The natural world also includes what lies beyond Earth, including our moon (Luna), other planets in our Solar System, the Sun, the Milky Way, and our entire

---

[12] Merriam-Webster. The natural world (2017). Retrieved from https://www.merriam-webster.com/dictionary/the%20natural%20world

Universe. If we discover that there are ways of acquiring empirical information about what lies beyond *our* Universe (i.e., in the Multiverse), then that could become subject to scientific study as well, but at present we are limited to studying our Universe.

So, science is a systematic study of the natural world, including the Universe, our Solar System, Earth, and everything on it, living or non-living. Tenet: To count as science, any prediction being studied must be able to be proven wrong (in principle, meaning that we may not have the technology to prove it wrong yet).

What does that exclude? If the natural world is the Universe and every physical thing in it, *is* there anything that isn't subject to scientific study? Yes. For example, if I say that the ability of Apple, Inc.'s "Siri" personal assistant to answer questions means that Siri possesses consciousness, that doesn't meet the criteria of a scientific question because there is no agreed-upon definition of consciousness, so the statement cannot be proven wrong. This example highlights the importance of being able to define your terms. Other examples include questions such as "is music so enjoyable because it connects us to the Universe on a mathematical level?", "does reading a poem or a novel put you literally in the mind of the author?" and "are humans basically good or basically bad?" None of these questions can be defined precisely enough to make them subject to scientific answers. Tenet That doesn't at all mean that they aren't questions worth discussing—one of the greatest joys of being human is the ability to engage in these sorts of philosophical discussions with each other (or to enjoy thinking about them within our own minds). Great insights might be found in considering these questions, and those insights may have great value on their own and might also lead to testable scientific hypotheses.

    The examples above have something in common: They have to do with statements about *thoughts*. Thoughts are interesting (as is consciousness, which is really a subset of "thoughts of awareness") because they are created by electrical and chemical interactions of ordinary matter (as far as we know), but they seem to somehow be greater than just interactions of matter. We rightly marvel at this, but the reason that thoughts and consciousness seem to be greater than the sum of their parts could be that we haven't seen mechanisms complex and subtle enough to produce such a result outside of ourselves. This perception may change as Artificial Intelligence (AI) becomes more convincing and harder to distinguish from human interaction.

Back to our discussion of science. It must be acknowledged that sometimes science gets it wrong with far-reaching, harmful consequences. One recent, long-lasting and continuing example is the consensus that emerged in the scientific community between 1970 and 1980, and then became enshrined in every aspect of life, that dietary fat and cholesterol were bad for you and should be avoided. Why has this been harmful? Because it led many (not just individuals, but also food manufacturers and government agencies) to make and recommend foods heavy in carbohydrates and sugar. If they were low-fat, they were thought to be healthier. We now know that a diet heavy in carbs and sugar is bad for us, and that fats can be beneficial because they can make us feel full longer and lead to less overeating. We have all this to thank for the exploding obesity crisis that continues to this day.

As I said, these misconceptions persist, so many people reading this right now are thinking, "Wait, what are you talking about? Fat and cholesterol *are* bad for you!" Well, it seems that they probably *aren't*–at least, according to *current* science [13, 14, 15]—though. Reading the articles noted in the footnote will show you the current science isn't in complete agreement, either.

Another example of the scientific and medical communities getting something completely wrong for a long time involves H. pylori (Helicobacter pylori). Doctors had been telling their patients for decades that their gastritis pain and peptic ulcers were being caused by stress and lifestyle choices. In 1982, however, Barry Marshall and Robin Warren discovered a microbial cause for these ailments: H. pylori. Dr. Marshall demonstrated and tested this by the unconventional and brave method of drinking it! The two were awarded the Nobel Prize in medicine for their discovery.

So, if science can get things so wrong, and the consequences of that can be so detrimental, why do we still use it and rely on it? Because of the *net positive*

---

[13] Merline, John, *Investor's Business Daily* (2016, April 18). How 'Settled Science' Helped Create A Massive Public Health Crisis. Retrieved from http://www.investors.com/politics/commentary/how-settled-science-caused-a-massive-public-health-crisis/
[14] Whoriskey, Peter, *The Washington* Post (2015, February 10). The U.S. government is poised to withdraw longstanding warnings about cholesterol. Retrieved from https://www.washingtonpost.com/news/wonk/wp/2015/02/10/feds-poised-to-withdraw-longstanding-warnings-about-dietary-cholesterol/?utm_term=.b2ba26f8dc60
[15] Merline, John, *Investor's Business Daily* (2015, October 7). Got Incompetence? The Federal Gov't Has Misled Public About Milk For Decades. Retrieved from http://www.investors.com/politics/commentary/government-advice-on-whole-milk-has-been-wrong/

that science has been and continues to be in all our lives. Because even though it sometimes gets things wrong, there are so many *overwhelming positives* that it has brought and continues to bring. What is probably thought to be the greatest harm caused by science? Even though there have been medical fiascos like the ones discussed above (and there will be more in the future—biology is very complex), I think it's safe to say that it's the creation of weapons of war. Just a little research reveals that science-based medicine and agriculture have saved more lives than war has ended. It's true: Estimates for the total number of people killed in wars throughout all human history range from 150 million (which honestly seems low to me) to one billion.[16] Now, lives saved by science-based medicine and agriculture:[17]

- Vaccinations: Over a billion
- Water chlorination: 175 million
- Antibiotics: 200 million
- Pasteurization of food: 250 million

---

[16] https://www.nytimes.com/2003/07/06/books/chapters/what-every-person-should-know-about-war.html#:~:text=Estimates%20for%20the%20total%20number,men%20away%20from%20their%20wives.

[17] https://aperioncare.com/blog/inventions-life-expectancy/

- The discovery and development of blood groups and blood transfusions: One billion
- Synthetic fertilizer: One billion

The list goes on and on. Science has been, and continues to be, *the greatest good* that humans have ever come up with, by any objective measure: Human life, freedom from disease and suffering and hunger—nothing else even comes close.

And I haven't even talked about the great truths, beauty, and wonders of the Universe, Earth, life and humanity that science has opened our eyes and our understanding to. The truth that the Earth is not at the center of the Universe, but revolves around the Sun, may seem obvious to us now, but it was one of the great scientific discoveries that taught us, perhaps, a little humility.

As Marie Curie said, "I am among those who think that science has great beauty." Who among us hasn't found beauty in the pictures captured by the Hubble Space Telescope and the James Webb Space Telescope?

As for wonders, there are too many to try to list, but here's one of my favorites:

Every atom that we are made of that is heavier than hydrogen and helium—all the carbon and oxygen and iron, and everything else, in *us*—was forged either inside of a star or in a collision of neutron stars. That's awe-inspiring!

Medicine. Food. Billions of lives saved. Truth, beauty, and wonder... quite a lot for one little method, wouldn't you say? *That's* why we continue to use science and rely on it.

Another reason that we continue to rely on the scientific method even though it sometimes gets things wrong is similar to why we continue with other major human institutions that are very difficult but indispensable, including, for example, democracy and capitalism. Democracy is fraught with dangers, but humanism includes the idea that people have the right and the responsibility to hold their governments accountable for their actions, which can only be accomplished through democracy. So, we don't abandon democracy; we put in place checks and balances to protect against its perils (the main one is majoritarianism, or the tyranny of the mob). Likewise, capitalism is not without its dangers (over-concentration of wealth, abuse of workers and disregard of harm to consumers and the environment), but that doesn't mean you completely get rid of capitalism. Capitalism provides an indispensable incentive for innovation and human progress, and it is fair that individuals should be able to profit from their effort and ingenuity. But the dangers are real, so it is necessary to put in place mechanisms to protect against its excesses, such as business regulations to protect workers, consumers, and the environment, and economic mechanisms for collectivism to ensure that everyone benefits from the greater capitalistic enterprise. The fact that these enterprises frequently get things wrong doesn't mean that they aren't worthwhile. It doesn't even mean that they aren't the *best alternatives* available. It is more a reflection of just how extremely complex governance and economics are. So it is with science: the subjects of scientific study, in particular the studies of biology and medicine, are exceedingly complex and difficult. It is easy to find mistakes made; that is how we are wired, to see problems. But it is important to also remember and give credit for the many successes of science and science-based medicine and agriculture, which are far too numerous to try to list (see these links for a sampling[18, 19]). The evidence seems overwhelming that science is, in

---

[18] Fact Monster. Life Changing Science Discoveries (2017). Retrieved from https://www.factmonster.com/science/general-science/life-changing-science-discoveries
[19] CDC. Ten Great Public Health Achievements in the 20th Century (2017). Retrieved from https://www.cdc.gov/about/history/tengpha.htm

fact, the *best alternative* available for learning about the natural world.

Science also has self-correcting mechanisms; they include the double-blind standard of studies (in which neither the scientists doing the study nor the subjects of the study know who is in the test group and who is in the control group[20]) and peer review practices insist that scientists who make a claim provide the rest of the scientific community with the details of how they obtained their results so that other scientists can try to replicate or refute their results.

Yes, science sometimes gets it wrong–very wrong. However, even in the extreme example of flawed nutrition science, how long did it take for it to start to correct itself? Thirty years. What corrected it? More science. What other global enterprise corrects itself so quickly? Yes, scientists are just as prone to human frailties, such as ego, pride and greed, that can lead to cognitive biases and even intentional deception, as anyone else. But you know what? So are all the practitioners of non-scientific approaches, such as "alternative" medicine. And science is the only

---

[20] When testing for efficacy of a new medication or other treatment, there is a "control group" that receives a placebo, and the double-blind practice ensures that outcomes cannot be influenced by either the clinician or the patient knowing who received the medication and who received the placebo, because they don't know.

knowledge-seeking enterprise that has mechanisms in place to discover and correct the errors that result from these inescapable human weaknesses. Tenet

Good Current Science, Outdated Science, and Pseudoscience

Differentiating between good current science, outdated science, and pseudoscience is not just an academic exercise—it has real-world consequences including causing many animals to die for no reason and even causing disease and death in humans. Tenet

Let's look at each in turn:

Good current science: The study was conducted according to proper protocols and was published in a well-known journal appropriate to its field and has been repeated by others competent in the field who reproduced the same results.

Example:

Some science, though not new, remains currently valid. A very instructive example is the germ theory of disease developed by Louis Pasteur in 1865. The theory, that many diseases are caused by microorganisms, has been supported by countless studies. It has also led to many more specific scientific studies that seek to find the specific cause of specific diseases. It also led to the development, in 1881, also by Pasteur, of inoculation by attenuated culture of microorganism (also known as vaccination).[21] It should be noted that just because information comes from what is judged to be "good science" does not necessarily mean that it is true—that said, it does mean that it has a higher likelihood of being true than information from other types of sources. Tenet There are many examples of science that were once thought to be good science that ended up being wrong.[22]

Outdated science: These are scientific theories which were considered valid in the past but have been replaced by new or more comprehensive theories and new technological tools.

Examples:

Classical elements—In ancient Greece, it was thought that all matter was formed of four elements: Earth, Air, Fire, and Water (similar theories existed in other parts of the ancient world, also). This is a good example of a theory

---

[21] Surendra Verma, *The Little Book of Scientific Principles, Theories, & Things* (Metro Books, 2006), 104.
[22] Freedman, David H., *Wrong: Why Experts* Keep Failing Us – And How to Know When Not to Trust Them* (Little, Brown, 2010) 231-238

being accepted because the technology didn't yet exist to show it to be false. It wasn't until the Scientific Revolution in the 1600s that empirical investigation began to undo this theory, with the final blow being dealt by Antoine Lavoisier's *Elements of Chemistry*, which included the first list of chemical elements, in 1789.

The Geocentric Universe (and the later Ptolemaic Model which attempted to account for irregularities in the motions of celestial objects being observed for the first time due to the invention of telescopes in the 1600s)–Since Aristotle in ancient Greece, it had been thought that the Earth was at the center of the Universe, with everything revolving around it. To an observer with no knowledge of the Earth's rotation this seemed to make sense at the time, and it fit with religious concepts of humanity being divinely created and occupying a special place in the Universe. However, the Heliocentric Universe theory, where the Sun is at the center of the Universe, made the observed orbits of the planets make more sense. The Heliocentric model would end up being replaced also, this time by the discovery of the Milky Way galaxy. It would then be discovered that many of the observed nebulae thought to be in the Milky Way are in fact other galaxies.

Pseudoscience: Non-scientific claims pretending to be scientific.

There are at least two subcategories of pseudoscience:

1. Making claims that are not scientific in nature but stating that they are supported by scientific evidence; and
2. Misconstruing and selectively citing scientific research results to support your position while ignoring the greater number of results that refute it.

Examples:

    A. Creationism (also known as "Creation Science")–By definition, Creationism states that the Universe and humanity were created by Divine processes, not natural processes, but then proponents of it try to use scientific "evidence" and terminology in support of it.

    B. Parents not having their children vaccinated because of fear due to a disproven publication and to general mistrust of government and industry. A study published in *The Lancet* (a medical journal in the United Kingdom) in 1998 linked the MMR vaccine (a common vaccine given to prevent Measles, Mumps, and Rubella) to autism. The study has since been discredited and the overwhelming consensus of the scientific, medical, and academic communities is that there is not any link between any vaccines and autism.

To be fair to the author of the study, he did not say not to vaccinate at all, he said to give the vaccinations one at a time. However, many parents, scared by the report, do not vaccinate at all, and the entire study was discredited.[23] Also, subsequent studies have indicated that it is actually safer to give the MMR vaccine than to split them up.[24] To be fair to proponents of a link between vaccinations and autism, there is a large cottage

---

[23] BBC News (2015, August 5). What's behind the 'anti-vax' movement? Retrieved from http://www.bbc.com/news/health-33774181
[24] CDC (2017, May 4). Measles, Mumps, and Rubella (MMR) Vaccine Safety. Retrieved from http://www.cdc.gov/vaccinesafety/vaccines/mmr-vaccine.html

industry of websites, publications, journalism, etc. devoted to supporting this link, and it is quite difficult to differentiate between the good sources and the bad. This is compounded if you don't trust government, academia, or the pharmaceutical industry.[25,26,27]

---

[25] Health Protection Surveillance Centre (2002, August 1). MMR versus Separate Single Vaccines for Measles, Mumps and Rubella. Retrieved from http://www.hpsc.ie/A-Z/VaccinePreventable/Vaccination/News/title-2031-en.html
[26] CDC. Science Summary: CDC Studies on Thimerosal in Vaccines (2017). Retrieved from http://www.cdc.gov/vaccinesafety/pdf/cdcstudiesonvaccinesandautism.pdf
[27] CDC. Vaccines Do Not Cause Autism, There is no link between vaccines and autism, and Vaccine ingredients do not cause autism (2017). Retrieved from http://www.cdc.gov/vaccinesafety/concerns/autism.html

Conspiracy Theories

The issue of mistrust of institutions—government, academia, and industry—that we should be able to rely on to seek and provide the truth, leads to many conspiracy theories, also called "parapolitics" by Joel Levy in his book *The Little Book of Conspiracies: 50 Reasons to Be Paranoid*. Numerous books are devoted to this subject, which is in itself a reason to be suspicious of the motivations of those who perpetrate conspiracy theories: there is money to be made by feeding into people's paranoia. Titles such as *You Are Being Lied To*, *Everything You Know is Wrong*, and *You Are Still Being Lied To* promise to let you in on the secrets, the Big Lies, and make you among the less gullible of us, which feels good and will, presumably, make you more intellectually attractive.

Conspiracy theories are interesting in that they often include a mix of pseudoscience and psychology that can make it very tempting for even highly educated and very intelligent people to question the overwhelming agreement of authorities on questions of medicine, politics, and science. The psychological components include the fact that sometimes these institutions *do* get caught lying to the public, so it is not so far-fetched to think that they may be lying in a particular case, and we don't want to be one of the naïve dupes that blindly believes whatever *they* tell us. On the other hand, being prone to believing conspiracy theories has also come to carry a negative stigma, so there are two competing psychological mechanisms at play.

We like feeling in control and we dislike uncertainty, so any complex question with no clear answer that carries emotional significance is a likely candidate for competing theories. It is important to note that the criterion "with no clear answer" seems to vary among individuals according to their knowledge and understanding of an issue and their biases. So, even with a topic for which the data is in and the consensus of the experts is near-universal, there are some people who are either unaware of the consensus, whose bias makes their mind impervious to being changed, or both. Unfortunately, this means that it is impossible to convince everyone, no matter how solid the evidence. This is made worse by the facts that:

- The people who hold onto these theories also constitute a market for the conspiracy theorists to sell books to

- The conspiracy theorists are motivated to come up with convincing arguments and even couch them in the language and trappings of science
- The nature of scientific research is that there is often such a great volume of data that it is easy for those with alternative theories to cherry-pick the data, ignoring what refutes their theories
- Scientists are motivated to be cautious in their conclusions, giving an inherent rhetorical advantage to those who are less cautious

It must also be acknowledged that sometimes the conspiracy theories turn out to be correct (or to have a high likelihood of being correct), which leads many to give credence to other conspiracy theories that aren't credible at all.

Here is a short list of conspiracy theories, taken from the above-mentioned book by Levy, with his determination of likelihood of validity and an assessment (his, mine, or a mix) of potential harm resulting from people believing them:

- AIDS being man-made to target certain vulnerable groups (Blacks, homosexual, drug user)—close to 0% chance of validity, has had severe detrimental impact by discouraging these groups from accepting treatment.

- Fluoridation of water (touted as preventing tooth decay) causing health problems and providing a corrupt means of disposing of pollutants—31% chance of validity, questionable but possible ongoing harm and fraud.
- A cancer cure exists but is being hidden from the public for the sake of profits—close to 0% chance of validity, harm includes patients seeking alternative medicine remedies while avoiding proven therapies and causing mistrust of the medical and pharmaceutical industry in general (which can lead to people seeking alternative remedies while avoiding proven therapies for other maladies as well).
- JFK was not assassinated by a lone gunman; Oswald was working with U.S. or Soviet covert ops or anti-Castro Cubans—44% chance of validity, no real impact on anyone directly, but fosters mistrust of government (whether this is a good thing or a bad thing can be debated).

There are many others, spanning myriad topics including medicine, science, politics, and science fiction. The point here is not to review them all, but to consider a few that are instructive. Of the four listed above, I find the cancer cure conspiracy theory to be the most relevant and far-reaching in its implications. The question of fluoridation of water seems to me to be worthy of further study. JFK-Oswald conspiracies are historical curiosities that make for good parlor-room discussions. Theories such as the AIDS conspiracy are indeed extremely detrimental and have tragic real-world consequences, but what is particularly harmful about the cancer cure conspiracy theory is that it implies the same question for any illness: do they have a cure that they are hiding from us to keep us sick so they can sell us more treatments?

Of course, human flaws, such as greed, fear and ego, as well as government and corporate corruption, can all play a part in motivations. However, remember that those same human motivations of greed and ego also serve to correct the negative influence. For every scientist motivated to hide the truth of the results of a study, there will be others that can make their careers by exposing it. Also remember that medical research isn't only being conducted in the U.S.–a conspiracy to hide a cure for cancer would require the collusion of *all* governments and *all* pharmaceutical companies and *all* universities worldwide–this is simply not realistic. That is part of the self-correcting nature of scientific progress (which includes medical research). It is far from perfect, but it is the *only* human enterprise that has such extensive mechanisms built in to expose the bad science over time.

Conspiracy theories have their place—they sometimes do expose corruption in government and industry. After all, unfair players *do* sometimes conspire to profit by deceiving us, and any exposé of that is, by definition, a conspiracy theory. Tenet: But remember that sometimes people conspire to deceive us by convincing us that they have uncovered a conspiracy—it is ironic, but true. Why would they do this? To sell product. Many people buy books and attend talks by these theorists, and some of the theorists also are selling products, such as homeopathic therapies to treat disease—this is a booming business, and an obvious incentive to conspire to deceive us.

Myriad examples of pseudoscience exist, and it is wise to be familiar with them, so you are not susceptible to deception. Tenet Here are some common ones:

- *Astrology*—The belief that the positions of celestial objects (planets, stars, constellations) can provide information about natural events and human affairs (including human personalities) here on Earth.

- *Wizardry and Witchcraft* – The belief that some people have magical powers and can make effects happen using an invocation or spell, but without a demonstrable mechanistic cause.
- *ESP (extrasensory perception), clairvoyance, fortune-telling and other psychic phenomena* – The belief that some people can perceive thoughts, see the future, talk with deceased spirits (the concept of "deceased spirits" is itself pseudoscience), etc. without any demonstrable mechanism (or any demonstrable effectiveness).
- *The killing of rhinos for their horns* due to false beliefs that their horns cure medical ailments. A similar example involves killing sharks for their fins for the same reason.
- *Healing powers of crystals* – The belief that many crystals have healing powers.
- *Faith healing* – The belief that some people can cure disease and injury by having faith in a divine power.
- *Telekinesis* – The belief that some people can move or alter physical objects with their thoughts.

  All these claims above can be tested, so they are scientifically falsifiable or verifiable.

Many have been tested many times, and none have been scientifically shown to work. There are always simpler explanations for observed effects, or else the reported effects cannot even be verified.[28] Therefore, they all are guilty of the logical fallacies of *Flawed Assumption* and *Affirming the Consequent* (see the Appendix), as well as violating all three of the basic axioms of science (see *Axioms of Science* chapter in this book).

There are also claims that are completely nonscientific in nature and therefore not subject to being judged as good science, obsolete science, nor pseudo-science. For example, many people believe in reincarnation. It is difficult to imagine a scientific test to disprove this and, if there is in fact no conceivable test to disprove it, then it is not a scientific claim. This does not mean it is right; just that it cannot be proven wrong. Does this mean that it is rational to believe it or even to allow for the possibility of it being true? Consider this: If you say that a phenomenon such as reincarnation should be considered valid, then why not allow any other claim with the same level of verifiability

---

[28] Sagan, Carl and Druyan, Ann, *The Demon-Haunted World: Science as a Candle in the Dark* (Ballantine Books, 1997), 3-14

to be considered valid? For example, a belief in tree spirits or human transference into animals (or even into plants or inanimate objects) should be considered equally valid. The only real difference is that the latter examples are more removed from our civilization in time. While many people today still believe in reincarnation, most of the peoples that believed in tree spirits and transference of the external human spirit into other entities lived long ago (or perhaps in a different culture than ours).[29] This is no doubt why these potential beliefs sound stranger to us today. Nonetheless, there are people who believe in reincarnation today, just as there are people who believe in life after death (a related belief) and heaven and hell (also related). All of these entail a belief in a human soul that can exist independently of a living body or that can transfer from one body to another. What is the basis of such beliefs, and what is the basis of believing that they are false? Can either of these claims (that these beliefs are true or that they are false) be *known* to be true? Let's look at the nature of knowledge to explore this.

---

[29] Frazer, Sir James George, *The Golden Bough: A Study in Magic and Religion* (1 Volume, Abridged Edition) (Simon & Shuster, 1985), 624-630

Epistemology

What do you mean when you say that you know something? Epistemology is the study of the origin, nature, scope and limitations of knowledge. It always faces the following question: How do we justify propositions (i.e., claims) as certain, probable, or false? In daily life, for example, we make life-and-death decisions every day based on probable outcomes (e.g., safe water, climate, serious surgeries, etc.). In general, you do not need to be 100% certain about something to be able to say, with credibility, that you know it.

All knowledge is subject to confirmation or refutation by the scientific method by which we continually confirm, revise or abandon old "truths" when warranted by new empirical data. Tenet "Truths" are natural and not supernatural in origin. For example, it was once widely held for a long time with absolute certainty that the Earth was at the center of the Universe and all human activity occurred on Earth. Scientific advances and the Sputnik launch proved these cases to be false.

Looking at another example, when spiritual mediums say that they can communicate with the dead, or when psychics say they can tell your future, be skeptical and then employ critical thinking, reliance on evidence, logic and reason, and the scientific method to evaluate the claim. Also remember that they are not (usually) offering to do so for free. They have a motivation to lie if doing so will profit them. Are there reasons to assume that claims of speaking to the dead or seeing the future are probably true? To really answer this, you must examine each specific claim individually.

First, stating that you can communicate with the dead assumes that there is life after death, which assumes that there is a human soul that can exist separately from a living body and that this soul will contain the memories and personality of the living person.

There are three assumptions:

1. Life after death.
2. Humans have souls that can exist separately from a living body.
3. This soul would contain the memories and personality of the now-dead person from when they were alive.

Assumption #2 is actually the one to start with, because the other two are *dependent* on that one being true. If you can refute that one, the others are also refuted.

Claim: There is a human soul that can exist separately from a living body.

There is a principle of philosophy called "animism" that states that all living things must possess a soul that gives them the vital force that is necessary for life because such a force cannot arise from non-living matter. However, since the Enlightenment and the Scientific Revolution, so much has been learned about how naturally occurring organic molecules can combine, how RNA and DNA and natural processes can guide reproduction, and even about how mental faculties in humans reside in specific parts of the brain and therefore also can arise from natural processes, that animism, though not precluded, is no longer necessary. Since it is not necessary, and since souls have never been observed, that claim that they exist must either be supported experimentally or discarded in favor of the simpler, abundant evidence that can explain how life emerges and personalities arise naturalistically.

Claim: Some people possess the ability to see the future or to see aspects of other peoples' lives to which they have never been privy.

There is another principle of philosophy that is supported by rationalism and naturalism, called "mechanism." Tenet: Mechanism states that "...natural phenomena can and should be explained by reference to matter and motion and their laws."[30] What this means to us in practice is that whenever someone makes a claim like this (that psychics can see the future), we should ask ourselves "What mechanism would make this possible?" If there is no obvious mechanism for it, then the onus (responsibility) of proof that it *can* occur is on those who say that it can or say that they can do it.

In every case of these classes of phenomena ever being scientifically tested by experimentation, the tests fail to confirm the claims.[31]

There are always simpler explanations. Mediums and psychics take advantage of some basics of psychology, common shared human experiences, trial and error, and people's strong desires to believe what they are saying even if they get some things wrong along the way. Even though people know that they are getting things wrong, they excuse the mistakes and still

---

[30] Encyclopedia Britannica. Mechanism (2017). Retrieved from https://www.britannica.com/topic/mechanism-philosophy
[31] Sagan, *The Demon-Haunted World*, 210-234

believe because it would force them to reexamine their whole worldview if they do not.

Because there is no evidence that can be demonstrated and tested empirically nor reason in support of the claims, the next question is whether there are other explanations that are more plausible. Note that, even if there weren't, it still wouldn't be evidence in favor of the claims—the onus of proof is still on the ones making the claim. As Carl Sagan was fond of saying, extraordinary claims require extraordinary evidence. He was right, and all these claims are extraordinary, and no credible evidence exists in favor of any of them.

If you wonder why these beliefs exist despite the fact that there are other, more plausible explanations for the observed events, remember that there weren't always more plausible explanations. For most of human history, we did not have the tools to figure these things out. It's only in the past 500 years or so that we have been making steady progress in answering questions that for hundreds of millennia were very mysterious.

The ability to *know* things has increased greatly in modern times, and this has contributed immensely to the improvement of human living conditions worldwide. The fact that there are still great problems does not negate this fact. The number of improvements made by scientific inquiry is ample evidence that we should continue to rely on science to seek further knowledge and progress. Tenet

Unfortunately, the ability to spread lies has also increased greatly through modern technology, and this can be used by self-serving interests to the detriment of humanity.

Agnotology

The promotion of lies and the hiding of truth. Agnotology is the study of, among other things, how we come to think that we "know" so many incorrect things, therefore being ignorant about the truth, and what we can do about it. A big part of how we come to think we know so many incorrect things turns out not to be by accident, but because there are people and organizations in the world that stand to benefit from deceiving us. We tend to think of ignorance as "missing knowledge," the absence of something—but ignorance can be manufactured, too—ignorance of good information is reinforced by seeding of bad information. Ignorance can also be reinforced simply by discrediting the source of existing good information.

Ignorance can be born and develop in so many ways. It is a natural tendency to keep secrets, for example, for many reasons. As kids, we learn to keep secrets to avoid getting in trouble, to create surprise for fun, and to create bonds of friendship. All these practices continue into adulthood. Businesses also keep secrets; we call them trade secrets, and they are usually considered ethical and necessary. The formula for your soft drink or even for your cigarette is valuable intellectual property, so of course you have a right to keep it a secret.

Sometimes, though, the ethical standing of such practices comes into question. What if you discover through your own research that your formula is harmful to your customers, and there would be no way to correct it without also significantly lessening the salability of your product, and therefore the profitability of your business and the value of your company's stock to your shareholders?

This is the main problem introduced by the construct of corporations. Because company officers are ethically required by fiduciary responsibility to serve the interests of their stockholders, ethical dilemmas are common. The basic dilemma is: do I serve my fiduciary duty to my stockholders, or do I serve my moral duty to the public? Both are considered ethical goods, and they can often collide. It doesn't require assuming an evil CEO to see how a company can make bad decisions sometimes (though sometimes vast economic incentive can certainly compromise one's ethics). The decisions can be difficult, and self-interest (indeed, self-preservation) can cloud thinking–CEOs can and do get fired for making morally-correct decisions that hurt the bottom line. Therefore, regulation of businesses is necessary; capitalism purists insist the only way for business to succeed is to get regulations out of the way and let the market (i.e., customers) reward and punish good and bad players. However, an understanding of this inherent ethical dilemma that arises out of the very construct of corporations, and the resulting incentives for disinformation (lies) made to customers carries too great a risk of secrecy and harm.

In addition to secrecy, other sources of ignorance include laziness and apathy, censorship of information, the fact that we forget so much information even when we do get it, and faith.[32] Note that "faith" here isn't meant just to mean faith in religious entities or institutions, though those are included, too. For example, people who have faith in a literal interpretation of *Genesis* may choose to remain ignorant of information about the age of the Earth. Many people also have faith in their governments to protect them and do the right thing, even if there is a history of learning after the fact that your government may have been dishonest about the reasons it gave for

---

[32]Proctor, Robert N. and Schiebinger, Londa, *Agnotology* (Stanford University Press, 2008), 2.

the actions it took (i.e., kept you ignorant about the true situation in your country or in the world).

Examples of agnotology:
Well-known examples include the big lies of the tobacco industry and climate change deniers, but there are many others, and new lies are being invented and perpetrated on the public all the time.

An important point is that the people who invent and perpetrate the lies often don't know they are lies. If you believe one big lie, that can spawn other lies.

Why are these lies created? Remember, there are people and organizations that have a vested interest in selling their message. That vested interest is either economic or political. To simplify, since all politics is ultimately about economics, it is always about money. Politicians need money to finance their campaigns, so they will often willingly perpetrate lies for industries and corporations that pay them to.

There are also many falsehoods that are perpetrated by people who believe them to be true and may not have any economic interest in spreading them—they simply believe that they are spreading the truth. They may even believe that they are doing good and protecting others. One example of this is the myth that irradiating food is harmful, when in fact it helps to protect consumers from illness and makes foods last longer before rotting. Similarly, chemical pesticides used in farming foods contribute less carcinogens to your diet than the plants themselves do. That's right— the plants themselves produce toxins to protect themselves from pests, but that doesn't mean we shouldn't eat them, and the toxins added in farming add even less toxicity than the plants that they are sprayed on already have in them. Both of these myths are very harmful. Millions die every year because of policies tied to baseless fears about pesticides (including DDT, which could save millions from death from malaria), and much illness and death from food poisoning could be prevented by irradiation of food. In both cases, people with good intentions continue to get it wrong, ignore the science, feed the public's fears, and spread false information that prevents the use of these safe and potentially beneficial technologies.[33]

These examples show that identifying false information isn't just an academic exercise, but has real, far-reaching and lifesaving (or death causing) implications.

---

[33] John Stossel, *Myths, Lies, and Downright Stupidity*, pp. 1-10

What about this book? Is it perpetrating lies? There will undoubtedly be some people that say that it does, because it contains material that some may find controversial. Some who say this will be lying to serve their own purposes, some may believe it when they say it because of other lies that they believed, and some will think this book is telling the truth. If someone else tells you that it is a lie (or tells you that it's the truth), ask yourself, "How might this person (or the organization that this person represents) benefit from telling me what to believe?" I have tried extremely hard to avoid perpetrating any lies in this book, both by trying to examine my own preconceived notions (cognitive biases) and by doing the research to try to be current with information. I freely acknowledge that I know that I will not have been perfect in either effort, but any bad information that remains is unintentional, and I will try to find it and correct it in the next edition. I hope that readers will point out errors to me when they find them and, if I agree* with the finding, I will update the information in the next edition. Of course, I do have an economic incentive to represent myself and my book as honest purveyors of knowledge, so you would be well-served by not taking my word for it, but by seeking out opinions of people who you trust, as well as forming your own opinion (hopefully, based on knowledge and research).

*I make this qualification because a reader may unintentionally or intentionally try to "correct" good information with bad, and I will of course not make changes based on such attempts.

Debunking Misinformation, Disinformation, Fake News, and Deep Fakes

Identifying misconceptions and lies by subjecting them to logic and science.

Debunking false information (agnotology) is fine, and we will do this here, but it is not enough to debunk a bunch of false beliefs if you will just go out and pick up a bunch of new ones–that's why it's also important to have the cognitive tools at your disposal to analyze new information (critical thinking) as well as to re-think old information that does not get debunked by others: you can and should be your own debunker. Tenet

Many fine resources exist for finding debunked bunk and for helping you to become a better debunker, and it is helpful to be familiar with them. The most well-known website is snopes.com, but I will provide some more resources here. Many are web sites, but there are also some excellent books that I recommend highly. See *For Further Reading* for a list.

Possibly the best of the books is Carl Sagan's *The Demon-Haunted World: Science as a Candle in the*

Dark. Sagan doesn't just address numerous misconceptions and pseudo-sciences—he does this, and probably better than anyone, but he does something much more important and useful: he teaches "the fine art of baloney detection," or, as I called it above, how to be your own debunker. In this chapter of his book, Sagan presents descriptions of logical fallacies, as I have done here in this chapter. He also discusses other "tools for skeptical thinking," including independent confirmation of facts, substantive debate by knowledgeable people on more than one side of a debate, the importance of measurement and quantification (where appropriate), and controlled experiments. Among the discredited myths in this wonderful book: faith healing, UFOs, clairvoyance (ESP, or Extra Sensory Perception), channeling (speaking with the dead), the healing powers of crystals, astrology, prophesy, and witchcraft. Sagan expertly debunks these large, timeless myths.

A good, current resource that I found recently is *Thinking is Power* (https://thinkingispower.com), created by Melanie Trecek-King, a biology professor who "... recognized the need for a general-education science course that focused less on facts and more on science as a way of knowing, so she created a novel course that uses pseudoscience, bad science, and science denial to engage students and teach science literacy, information literacy and critical thinking." As a sample from her site, here is a useful list of *Characteristics of Pseudoscience*:[34]

1. Is UNFALSIFIABLE (can't be proven wrong): Makes vague or unobservable claims
2. Relies heavily on ANECDOTES, personal experiences, and testimonials
3. CHERRY PICKS confirming evidence while ignoring/minimizing disconfirming evidence
4. Uses TECHNOBABBLE: Words that sound scientific but don't make sense
5. Lacks PLAUSIBLE MECHANISM: No way to explain it based on current knowledge
6. Is UNCHANGING: Doesn't self-correct or progress
7. Makes EXTRAORDINARY/EXAGGERATED CLAIMS with insufficient evidence
8. Professes CERTAINTY: Talks of "proof," with great confidence
9. Commits LOGICAL FALLACIES: Arguments contain errors in reasoning

---

[34] Retrieved from
https://thinkingispower.com/?s=characteristics+of+pseudoscience
September 7, 2024. Reprinted with permission.

10. Lacks PEER REVIEW: Goes directly to the public, avoiding scientific scrutiny
11. Claims there's a CONSPIRACY to suppress their ideas

A good book for debunking more contemporary, topical myths and pseudoscience is the aforementioned *Myths, Lies, and Downright Stupidity*, by John Stossel. In addition to the myths of the dangers of many pesticides and food irradiation discussed above, Stossel takes on many other topics,* including:

- Gender-related myths (an entertaining chapter)
- Myths about modern business practices (I don't agree with all of his conclusions, but it is good to consider other perspectives and arguments)
- Government, politics, and economics
- Education and schools
- Consumer goods
- Law and tort
- Health
- Numerous "urban myths" and pseudoscience claims

- Marriage, psychology, and even some philosophy

* Many of his discussions are exclusively about the United States.

Don't Believe Everything You Think, by Thomas Kida, explores in depth some common errors that we all make in thinking. Being aware of these can help to recognize when we make these mistakes and sometimes can help us to correct ourselves.

The six cognitive "mistakes" include:
- Preferring stories to statistics
- Seeking information that confirms what we already think (confirmation bias)
- Not recognizing how chance and coincidence affect events
- Misperceiving reality
- Oversimplifying
- The unreliable nature of memory

Why People Believe Weird Things, by Michael Shermer, who publishes *Skeptic* magazine and is the director of the *Skeptics Society*, advocates for science and skepticism and directly debunks the following:
- Paranormal and pseudoscientific claims, including claims of glimpses of afterlife in

near-death experiences, alien abductions, and witch hunts
- Creationism
- Holocaust denial

I also like his analysis, at the end, of the answer to the question of why we believe the weird things we believe. Essentially, because we want to. I would add that we want to *because it's easier*, but it is far less rewarding than figuring out the reality.

How We Know What Isn't So, by Thomas Gilovich, is an excellent examination of how we come to form false beliefs, why this is so harmful (one reason is that erroneous beliefs crowd out the truth), how we know they are wrong, and what we can do about it.

Debunking Resources On The Internet:

Note: Some of these aren't, strictly-speaking, "debunking" sites—some are just references to help you debunk things the old-fashioned way: through researching them.

General:

https://www.refseek.com/directory/

https://www.snopes.com/

http://www.factcheck.org/hot-topics/

https://www.truthorfiction.com/

Science:

http://www.skeptical-science.com/critical-thinking/top-5-fact-checking-websites/

https://blog.disqus.com/vote-the-top-10-best-science-websites

https://badscidebunked.wordpress.com/

http://www.factcheck.org/scicheck/

http://www.businessinsider.com/worst-science-health-myths-2016-1/#th-sugar-and-chocolates-are-aphrodisiacs-14

https://thinkingispower.com/

Medicine:

https://www.nih.gov/

https://www.cdc.gov/

www.webmd.com/

https://www.refseek.com/directory/health_medical.html

https://linksmedicus.com/medical-specialties/?gclid=EAIaIQobChMI6_Hw6bKx1wIV27bACh0QgwvKEAMYAyAAEgKp9fD_BwE

https://www.uptodate.com/home

https://www.ncbi.nlm.nih.gov/pubmed

http://www.jstor.org/

Internet Hoaxes:

https://www.techrepublic.com/blog/10-things/top-10-sites-to-debunk-internet-hoaxes/
(list of sites)

Political Fact Checking:

https://www.dailydot.com/layer8/best-fact-checking-websites/

http://politifact.com/

FactCheck.org

https://www.washingtonpost.com/news/fact-checker/

https://www.opensecrets.org/

Fake News:

http://www.factcheck.org/2017/07/debunking-fake-news/?gclid=EAIaIQobChMIqc_BvKex1wIVw7XACh1Z_gnyEAMYASAAEgL-A_D_BwE

https://www.ifla.org/publications/node/11174?gclid=EAIaIQobChMI-sX1prWx1wIVirjACh2R4g9wEAAYBCAAEgKe5_D_BwE

https://www.npr.org/sections/alltechconsidered/2016/12/05/503581220/fake-or-real-how-to-self-check-the-news-and-get-the-facts

https://docs.google.com/document/d/10eA5-mCZLSS4MQY5QGb5ewC3VAL6pLkT53V_81ZyitM/edit (contains a terrific list of sites with ratings, such as "fake," "satire," "hate," "unreliable," "junksci" and "unknown.") This snapshot is somewhat disheartening when you look at how few sites are marked as "reliable."

AI (Artificial Intelligence), fakes, and deepfakes deserve special mention. Some helpful tips and resources for detecting fakes and deepfakes include:

- Check the URL of news stories. washingtonpost.com is a legitimate URL, but washingtonpost.com.co is not. It has been used to spread fake news and contains clickbait to other bogus news sites. Note that these sites are in flux, new ones pop up all the time, and many go away after awareness of their illegitimacy makes their continued usefulness untenable. See https://en.wikipedia.org/wiki/List_of_fake_news_websites for a list that is updated by the public regularly. This is one instance where Wikipedia is actually a great source.
- If you see a purported quote from someone who is well-known, search it. You should be able to track it to an event or an official statement if it is valid.
- For images, you can do a reverse search on Google: right-click the image (or tap & hold on mobile), copy the URL, and go to images.google.com to find out where it came from. Then, see the resources above to find if the site is legitimate or not. I have heard that https://tineye.com/ is even better than Google at spotting fakes.

Conclusions & Recap

Now that we have considered principles of logic and logical fallacies; types of causes and effects; axioms of science; the scientific method; differentiating between good current science, outdated science, and pseudoscience; conspiracy theories; agnotology (the nature of misinformation); and debunking (how to identify and disprove misinformation), we have a solid foundation for analyzing information with guidelines that help us to ensure that we are not just engaging in wishful or magical thinking that may be emotionally satisfying, but to try to arrive at answers that more accurately reflect the real world and actual events.

In *Critical Thinking*, we discussed the importance of being skeptical, cognitive flaws we are all susceptible to, and types of reasoning. In *Principles of Logic and Logical Fallacies* (don't forget to see the Appendix for a very detailed listing of types of logical fallacies with examples), we looked at the structure of arguments and logical fallacies. With *Types of Causes and Effects*, we reviewed how events are causally linked (and how to consider if they really are at all) and different types of causes.

From there, after building a foundation of principles of rationality, we moved on to *Axioms of Science, The Scientific Method*, and *Differentiating Between Good Current Science, Outdated Science, and Pseudoscience*. In *Axioms of Science*, we talked about why the scientific method needs a foundation of truths that are accepted as factual and self-evident. In *The Scientific Method*, we discussed what the scientific method is, why it works, a bit of its history, and its limitations. In *Differentiating Between Good Current Science, Outdated Science, and Pseudoscience*, we looked at what makes good science (there is certainly bad science done), examples of outdated science, and types of pseudo-science.

We discussed agnotology, the promotion of lies and the hiding of truth, and how we come to think that we "know" so many incorrect things, therefore being ignorant about the truth, and what we can do about it. A big part of how we come to think we know so many incorrect things turns out not to be by accident, but because there are people and organizations in the world that stand to benefit from deceiving us.

Finally, we looked at debunking, how we can and should be able to do it for ourselves, and some common resources that can help us to debunk misinformation and disinformation.

Remember that you don't need to reread entire chapters (though it doesn't hurt). You can look through the Tenets at the end of the book to be reminded of the central premises of critical thinking.

I know it takes time to check things for accuracy, but the forces that want to trick us are so many and well-funded, the technology for tricking us is so good (and only getting better), and the potential consequences of us being tricked are so dire that it is not only worth it, but I would also say that it is imperative. The potential consequences cannot be stated too strongly: Not only can you personally be tricked into giving up your identity or your money, if we as a people are tricked into believing that a political leader said or did something that didn't actually happen, we may well elect the corrupt person and the leader that would have been good for us would lose. Yes, there have always been these kinds of dangers, low-tech things like other leaders simply telling lies. But the Internet helps lies to spread much faster, and AI makes it much harder to detect the lies. The Pew Research Center conducted a study wherein they canvassed experts in tech on an array of questions related to the *Future of The Internet* called *Experts Predict More Digital Innovation by 2030 Aimed at Enhancing Democracy*. In it, the authors describe misinformation as "pervasive, potent, problematic" and expressed concern about "how users will sort through fact and fiction."[35] There are some who hope for future tech-based solutions, but ours are the generations that are tasked with guiding us through this very difficult transition from a pre-Information Age/Artificial Intelligence (IA/AI) world into a much different and more perilous post-IA/AI world.

Plus, critical thinking is not only useful for identifying misinformation, disinformation, fake news, and deep fakes, but it also helps us to think more soundly in all aspects of life. It can help you communicate more effectively, make better decisions, and be better at your job or other hustle.

---

[35] Experts Predict More Digital Innovation by 2030 Aimed at Enhancing Democracy, Emily A. Vogels, Lee Rainie, and Janna Anderson, Pew Research Center, June 30, 2020. Retrieved from https://www.pewresearch.org/internet/2020/06/30/experts-predict-more-digital-innovation-by-2030-aimed-at-enhancing-democracy/ Aug. 23, 2024

Tenets of Critical Thinking

1. There are many vested interests that can profit from disseminating bad information (usually by making money off us or by keeping themselves in power).
2. Being able to question and analyze information is probably the most important skill that anyone can have now, and we should teach ourselves and our children the tools for this.
3. As expressed by Francis Bacon in his "Novum Organum" in 1620, "Whether or no (sic) anything can be known, can be settled not by arguing, but by trying."
4. Don't believe everything you hear, read, see, etc. (be skeptical). Use critical thinking, research and experimentation.
5. In critical thinking, the focus is on *how to* think, not *what to* think.
6. A proper education includes being equipped with critical thinking skills, and it is the duty of all parents (or guardians or caregivers) to do their best to assure that their kids have a proper education, and to themselves provide the aspects

of a necessary education that their children's schools fail to provide.

7. We can and should use these analytical tools not just with the statements of others, but our own, as well.

8. A logical argument always follows some version of the structure: *Assumption(s) + Evidence = Conclusion*. For a conclusion to be valid, the following must all hold up to scrutiny: The *assumption(s)* must be valid, and the *evidence* must be supported as factual (the logical premise connecting the assumptions and the evidence to the conclusion must be valid).

9. Logic is a necessary component of critical thinking, but it is not always sufficient. Some knowledge cannot be deduced from argument alone; we must test our theories and see if they hold up to scientific scrutiny. The scientific method is more reliable than the use of pure reason to arrive at what is true.

10. There are basic assumptions (axioms) in science that are accepted universally:

There are natural causes for events.

A few corollaries can be deduced and are important to state, since the temptations to break them are so common:

- If you can't identify a natural cause for an event, that doesn't mean that one doesn't exist. It may be just that you didn't know where to look or because one hasn't been found yet (and perhaps will be in the future).
- If you can't identify a natural cause for an event, that doesn't imply the necessity of a magical entity (e.g., a deity) to cause it.

Naturalistic evidence should be used to explain those events.

Cause and effect relationships in the world operate consistently and predictably.

- An example of what it means to say that these are axiomatic is that, if you conduct an experiment more than once and you get differing results, that doesn't mean that C is incorrect, it means that there was a difference in how the experiments were conducted.

11. The scientific method is the most reliable method of discovering how natural phenomena work.
12. Correlation does not imply causation.
13. Even the social sciences have embraced evidence-based practice to employ principles of the scientific method to affect the greatest good. In these ways and others, morally-sound ethics can be derived from science.
14. We all do science all the time, mostly without realizing it.
15. To count as science, any prediction being studied must be able to be proven wrong (in principle, meaning that we may not have the technology to prove it wrong yet).
16. There are phenomena that cannot be defined precisely enough to be subject to scientific answers, such as statements about thoughts (including consciousness).
17. Science is the only knowledge-seeking enterprise that has mechanisms in place to discover and correct the errors that result from inescapable human weaknesses.
18. Differentiating between good current science, outdated science, and pseudoscience is not just

an academic exercise—it has real-world consequences, including causing many animals to die for no reason, and even causing disease and death in humans.

19. Just because information comes from what is judged to be "good science" does not necessarily mean that it is true—that said, it does mean that it has a higher likelihood of being true than information from other types of sources.
20. Sometimes people conspire to deceive us by convincing us that they have uncovered a conspiracy.
21. There are numerous examples of pseudoscience, and it is wise to be familiar with them, so you are not susceptible to deception.
22. You can and should be your own debunker of the various kinds of false information.

For Further Reading

The Demon-Haunted World: Science as a Candle in the Dark (1997)
by Carl Sagan and Ann Druyan

The Little Blue Thinking Book: 50 Powerful Principles for Clear and Effective Thinking (2010)
by Brandon Royal

On Being Certain: Believing You Are Right Even When You're Not (2009)
by Robert A. Burton

The Little Book of Conspiracies: 50 Reasons to Be Paranoid (2005)
by Joel Levy and Kenneth Thomas

Proofiness: How You're Being Fooled by the Numbers (2011)
by Charles Seife

Sleight of Mind (2006)
by George A. Ulett

Agnotology: The Making and Unmaking of Ignorance (2008)
by Robert N. Proctor and Londa Schiebinger

Myths, Lies, and Downright Stupidity (2006)
by John Stossel

The Drunkard's Walk: How Randomness Rules Our Lives (2009)
by Leonard Mlodinow

Wrong: Why experts* keep failing us--and how to know when not to trust them *Scientists, finance wizards, doctors, relationship gurus, celebrity CEOs, high-powered consultants, health officials and more (2010)
by David H. Freedman

Intellectual Virtue: Perspectives from Ethics and Epistemology (2007)
by Michael DePaul and Linda Zagzebski

Don't Believe Everything You Think: The 6 Basic Mistakes We Make in Thinking (2006)
by Thomas E. Kida

Predictably Irrational, Revised and Expanded Edition: The Hidden Forces That Shape Our Decisions (2010)
By Dan Ariely

Bad Astronomy: Misconceptions and Misuses Revealed, from Astrology to the Moon Landing "Hoax" (2002)
by Philip C. Plait

The Book of Animal Ignorance: Everything You Think You Know Is Wrong (2008)
by John Mitchinson and John Lloyd

The Splendid Feast of Reason (2001)
by S. Jonathan Singer

Everything You Know Is Wrong: The Disinformation Guide to Secrets and Lies (2002)
by Russ Kick

You Are Being Lied To: The Disinformation Guide to Media Distortion, Historical Whitewashes and Cultural Myths (2001)
by Russ Kick

You Are STILL Being Lied To: The NEW Disinformation Guide to Media Distortion, Historical Whitewashes and Cultural Myths (Disinformation Guides) (2009)
by Russ Kick

How We Know What Isn't So: The Fallibility of Human Reason in Everyday Life (1993)
by Thomas Gilovich

Appendix: Logical Fallacies

LOGICAL FALLACIES:[36],[37],[38],[39],[40],[41]

Equivocation—Using words with ambiguous or multiple meanings to lead to an unsupported conclusion.

Examples:

It isn't nice to say that you are "critiquing" someone's speech, because being critical isn't nice. However, even though the two words share a common root, they have different meanings—being critical is negative; critiquing is providing a detailed analysis, which can include both positive and negative elements.

Since there are laws of nature, and laws are dictated by someone, that implies a lawgiver (a

---

[36] Royal, The Little Blue Thinking Book, 159-169.
[37] Williamson, Owen M. (2017). Master List of Logical Fallacies. Retrieved from http://utminers.utep.edu/omwilliamson/ENGL1311/fallacies.htm
[38] Gass, Robert, California State University, Fullerton (2017). Common Fallacies In Reasoning. Retrieved from http://commfaculty.fullerton.edu/rgass/fallacy3211.htm
[39] Weber, Ryan and Brizee, Allen (2013, March 11). Logical Fallacies. Retrieved from https://owl.english.purdue.edu/owl/resource/659/03/
[40] The Writing Center, University of North Carolina at Chapel Hill (2017). Fallacies. Retrieved from http://writingcenter.unc.edu/handouts/fallacies/
[41] Many of the examples offered are taken from or inspired by examples on https://www.logicallyfallacious.com

god). Actually, the word "law" has multiple meanings, and this usage means regularly occurring and apparently inevitable in nature, with no reference to a lawgiver.

Distinction Without a Difference—Using a different word with the same meaning or describing a situation that is factually different but logically the same.

Examples:

We can't judge his words by what people think he means; only by what he says. Since the meaning of his words cannot be established without thinking about them, this is a meaningless distinction.

Whether a group of insurgents are called rebels or freedom fighters depends only on your point of view of them as being against your ally or your foe. They are still an organized group fighting against the established power base.

Hasty Generalization—Making a claim about a group with a flawed sample.

Examples:

I don't think smoking is bad for you; my dad smoked his whole life and he lived to be 95. A sample of one is rarely enough to draw a conclusion.

I know a woman who used acupuncture while trying to get pregnant, and she succeeded. Therefore, acupuncture helps women get pregnant. What if another woman used acupuncture while trying to get pregnant and failed? Would you then conclude that acupuncture is effective as a contraceptive?

He has won four of the last five poker hands, therefore he is a good player. Maybe he's just been lucky—wait for 100 hands to play out before you judge.

Circular reasoning (also called a tautology)—Basing your conclusion on an assumption that depends on the conclusion being true.

Examples:

I am a better driver than any woman because I am a man and men are better drivers than women. God is real because the Bible says so and the Bible is the word of God, who is inerrant. This argument essentially says that God is real because God is real. There may be other reasons, that you find compelling, to believe that God is real, but this one is logically fallacious.

Fallacy of Negative Proof–Stating that your conclusion must be true because it has not been proven false (or the other way around).

Examples:

The magician levitated that person because you can't offer another convincing explanation. Just because he is skillful at his deceptions doesn't mean they aren't deceptions. Also, just because I am not personally knowledgeable enough on this subject to offer an explanation isn't evidence that there isn't an explanation.

No one can say what caused the Big Bang, so that whole theory falls. That's like saying that if we had no record of Christopher Columbus departing for his trip to the New World, it never happened. In both cases, there is ample evidence even without 100% complete evidence. Saying that something must be false because you can't prove it to be true is just as fallacious as saying it must be true because you can't prove it false.

Ad Hominem—Stating that a claim cannot be true because of who stated it, attacking the believability of the person making the argument, instead of the argument itself. The Poisoning the Well fallacy and the Tu Quoque fallacy are both special cases of the Ad Hominem fallacy

> Example: We can't believe what Al Gore says about global warming; he is a raging liberal who just wants to advance liberal policies. He may be a raging liberal and he may want to advance liberal policies, but that has no logical impact on the truth or lack of truth of his claims.

Poisoning the Well—A preemptive Ad Hominem attack, where the attacker impugns the character (or reliability, or whatever other quality that is pertinent) of the other person before the other person has even spoken.

> Example: The defendant was described by the prosecutor as a dishonest criminal; therefore, I won't believe a word he says. If you judge the truth of what the defendant says based on your

"well" being poisoned by what the prosecutor said, you are committing this fallacy.

Tu Quoque ("you, too")–Saying that someone's argument isn't valid because they don't follow the conclusions of it themselves.

> Example: Son, don't smoke–it's bad for you (said by a smoker). Attacking the validity of the statement "[smoking] is bad for you" because it was said by a smoker would be a tu quoque fallacy–it can still be true even if the speaker is being hypocritical.

Irrelevancy–Attacking a claim with arguments that are not directly related to the claim. Irrelevancy fallacies include the Non-Sequitur, Red Herring, and Wishful Thinking fallacies.

Non-Sequitur (doesn't follow)–Making a conclusion that is not logically connected to the premise or the argument.

> Example: The reason we see so much violence these days is because we live in a Godless society. This statement actually has more than one logical fallacy in it, but the non-sequitur is that it

simply doesn't follow that societies with less religion have more violence. Some of the least religious societies have the least violence, and some of the most religious societies have the most violence.[42]

Red Herring (beside the point)—Redirecting the argument to another issue that you feel better able to debate.

Example: If you say that the biblical account of creation cannot be true because it says that the Earth is only 6,000 years old, but we know from measurements of the expansion of the Universe that it is over 13 billion years old, and your friend says "Well, there is debate about that 6,000 number—some scholars say that the Bible actually indicates an age of 10,000 years," your friend is using a red herring fallacy to try to divert the conversation.

---

[42] Zuckerman, Phil, Los Angeles Times (2017). Think religion makes society less violent? Think again. Retrieved from http://www.latimes.com/opinion/op-ed/la-oe-1101-zuckerman-violence-secularism-20151101-story.html

Wishful Thinking (cognitive bias)–Evaluating an issue based more on what you want to be true than on the evidence.

> Example: When you believe that your candidate or your party is being truthful or has the best ideas just because you want this to be so, you are committing the wishful thinking fallacy.

Appeal to Authority–Because an expert says so, it must be true.

> Examples:
>
> Aristotle stated that heavier objects fall faster than lighter ones. This was accepted for almost 2,000 years before Galileo disproved it by experiment.
>
> Albert Einstein said that light will be bent when passing a massive object. Einstein was one of the smartest scientists to have ever lived, so this must be true. That would be fallacious thinking. The scientific community did not commit this fallacy. Even though Einstein said this and even though he provided sound arguments, the fact of

this was not accepted until proven true by experiments.

Appeal to Public Opinion—Claiming that an argument must be true because many people think that it's true. This is a special case of Appeal to Authority, where the public is seen as the authority.

Examples:

There was a time when most people thought that the world was flat. This seemed to make sense based on available data, and that's what everyone thought, but further scientific research would show it to be wrong.

It was once widely held that "bad air" caused diseases. It wasn't until Pasteur developed the germ theory of disease in the late 1800s that this popular opinion faded.

Doctors (and everyone else) believed that ulcers were caused by stress. It wasn't until the 1980s that it was discovered that the bacterium H. pylori causes ulcers.

Fallacy of Tradition—Claiming that an argument must be true because it has been that way for a long time.

This is a special case of Appeal to Authority, where the tradition and our ancestors are the authority.

> Example: Marriage has traditionally been between one man and one woman; therefore, same-sex marriage is immoral. This doesn't make same-sex marriage immoral; it just makes it non-traditional. Incidentally, this example also commits the fallacy of non-sequitur.

Flawed Assumption—Basing an argument on unsupportable claims. Flawed Assumption fallacies include the Fallacy of False Alternatives, Fallacy of the Golden Mean, Fallacy of Composition, Fallacy of Division, Fallacy of the Continuum, Incorrect Attack on a Generalization, Straw Man, Faulty Analogy, Cause and Effect, Slippery Slope Fallacy, Gambler's Fallacy, and Fallacy of False Precision.

Fallacy of False Alternatives (all or nothing fallacy)— When fewer alternatives are presented than actually exist (usually thought of as either *a* or *b* when more than two choices exist, but there can be any number; the important part is that some valid options are left out).

> Example: You're either with us or against us. It is possible to be either apathetic or ambivalent.

Fallacy of the Golden Mean—States that there is a compromise between any two options, and this must be the correct conclusion.

> Example: I ask for $20,000 for my car, which is the book value. You lowball me with an offer of $10,000 and then offer to split the difference and agree on a price of $15,000. "It's only fair," you say. No, it isn't.

Fallacy of Composition—Saying that because a component of a thing has (or lacks) a property, then the thing as a whole has (or lacks) it.

> Example: The human brain is made of atoms, which we agree lack consciousness; ergo, your brain cannot be the source of consciousness. This argument ignores the fact that when you combine different kinds of atoms, properties emerge that don't exist for any individual atom.

Fallacy of Division—Saying that because something possesses a property, all its component parts also have that property (this is the inverse of the Fallacy of Composition).

> Example: The Catholic Church is guilty of child molestation and coverups, therefore the priest at my local church is a child molester. It is logically fallacious (not to mention morally wrong) to accuse someone of being a criminal because others at their organization are guilty.

Fallacy of the Continuum—Saying that you cannot distinguish two related extremes because you can't identify the exact point where *a* changed to *b*.

> Example: Speciation is a perfect example of this. If you want to look at where your ancestors stopped being members of the species that directly preceded ours and started being members of Homo sapiens sapiens, you can't identify a single generation and say, "there: the parents were a different species, and the children are clearly Homo sapiens sapiens." Speciation doesn't work that way; it is a gradual accumulation of new traits that can take many generations. After enough generations, though, you would be able to say that this ancestor,

removed by x generations, is clearly of a different species.

Incorrect Attack on a Generalization—Saying that a generalization isn't true because you can find an exception or exceptions.

> Example: Wearing automobile safety belts isn't necessary because sometimes people die in car accidents because they were wearing their safety belt. Yes, there may be times when you would be better off without it on, but the odds greatly favor wearing them.

Strawman (or Straw Man)—Misrepresenting your opponent's argument so you can attack the distorted position you created, not the actual statement.

> Example: If someone running for office says that he doesn't believe in God, and his opponent says, "How can you vote for him? He thinks humans have no purpose and that morals don't exist." The opponent grossly mischaracterized and distorted the statement, even to the point of outright lying (to be charitable, sometimes Strawmen are created unintentionally—it is possible that the opponent truly believes that

atheism implies those things). It is a Strawman, nonetheless.

Faulty Analogy—Using a weak analogy to prove an argument.

> Example: Saying that life arose from inanimate matter is like saying that if you put a bunch of monkeys in a room and wait long enough, you will get the complete works of Shakespeare. This is a weak analogy because the monkeys are, presumably, hitting keys completely at random, while the ways that matter interact are not random (there are constraints imposed by laws of physics and chemistry, and we see structure emerge spontaneously in nature).

Slippery Slope Fallacy—Saying that a minor initial event will inevitably lead to a series of events that culminates in a major result.

> Example: If we allow gay people to get married, bestiality will ultimately result.

Gambler's Fallacy—Believing that past events affect future outcomes in random events.

Example: If a coin is flipped 10 times and is heads all 10 times, the next flip is more likely to be tails. The coin has no memory of how many times it has been heads.

Consider this: What if you put the coin down and wait a minute. Is it still more likely to be tails when you flip it? What is you wait an hour? A year? If you think that it now will be equally likely to be heads as tails, why? At what point did the odds reset? What mechanism controlled that?

Cause and Effect Fallacies: Post Hoc Ergo Procter Hoc, Cum Hoc Ergo Propter Hoc, Fallacy of Affirming the Consequent, and Fallacy of Denying the Antecedent

Post Hoc Ergo Procter Hoc—Probably the most common confusion of thinking that correlation implies causation (it doesn't), this fallacy says that because *b* followed *a* (in time), *a* caused *b*. A third factor could be involved, or one event following the other could be coincidence.

Example: I went out in the cold without a jacket, and I got sick. Therefore, being cold gave me a cold. Actually, a virus causes getting a cold, not body temperature.

Cum Hoc Ergo Propter Hoc—Very similar to the Post Hoc Ergo Procter Hoc fallacy, this one states that because *a* and *b* occurred at the same time, *b* caused *a* (or that *a* caused *b*). Again, correlation doesn't imply causation. Causation could be the reverse of what you assume, a third factor could be involved, or the two events occurring at the same time could be coincidence.

> Example: Since many gay people get AIDS, being gay causes AIDS. We know that the HIV virus causes AIDS, not sexual preference.

Fallacy of Affirming the Consequent—Assuming that since an effect sometimes follows a cause, when the effect happens, the cause must have also happened. Note the "sometimes"—the effect sometimes follows the cause, so if you only observe the effect, you can't conclude that the cause happened—maybe it was a different cause this time.

> Example: Your husband always gets you flowers after he does something wrong. He just got you flowers—he must have done something wrong. Even though he always gets you flowers after he does something wrong, that doesn't mean that doing something wrong is always the cause of him getting you flowers.

Fallacy of Denying the Antecedent—Assuming that since an effect sometimes follows a cause, when the effect did not happen, the event that ordinarily would cause the effect also did not happen. Again, note the "sometimes." The event that sometimes causes the effect could have still happened; it just didn't cause the effect this time.

> Example: Drawing on the previous example, maybe your husband did do something wrong, he just didn't get you flowers this time.

This list of fallacies is just one list, and it is a partial list at that—there are other lists that are more extensive, and others that are less so. If interested, please check out the cited resources for more. Learning more about logical fallacies makes watching politicians and pundits on TV much more entertaining. Just remember to try to subject your own party and its members to the same logical scrutiny that you do the opposition (as difficult as that can be, because we have to challenge our own cognitive biases).

Glossary

Agnotology: The study of culturally induced ignorance or doubt, particularly through the spread of misinformation.
Argument: A set of statements or propositions used to persuade others or provide reasons for accepting a conclusion.
Artificial Intelligence (AI): Computer systems capable of performing complex tasks that historically only a human could do, such as reasoning, making decisions, or solving problems.
Astrology: The belief that the movements and relative positions of celestial bodies can have an influence on human affairs and the natural world.
Axioms of Science: Basic principles accepted as self-evidently true, forming the foundation of scientific reasoning.
Big Bang: The rapid expansion of matter from a state of extremely high density and temperature that, according to current cosmological theories, marked the origin of the (our) Universe.
Big Lie, The: A gross distortion or misrepresentation of the facts, especially when used as a propaganda device by a politician or official body.
Burden of Proof: The obligation to prove one's assertion in a debate or argument.
Causal Chain: A series of events linked by cause-and-effect relationships.
Causation: The relationship between cause and effect, where one event leads to another.
Claim: An assertion that something is true or factual, typically supported by evidence.
Cognitive Bias: Systematic patterns of deviation from rationality in judgment.

Confirmation Bias: The tendency to search for or interpret information in a way that confirms one's preexisting beliefs.
Conspiracy Theory: A belief that some secret but influential organization is responsible for an event or phenomenon.
Correlation: A mutual relationship or connection between two variables.
Creationism: The belief that the Universe, the Sun and the planets, and the various forms of life were created by God out of nothing (ex nihilo).
Critical Thinking: The process of analyzing, evaluating, and synthesizing information to form a reasoned judgment.
Debunking: The process of exposing false claims or beliefs.
Deep Fakes: Media that use artificial intelligence to replace the likeness of one person with another in images, audio, or video.
Disinformation: False information spread deliberately to deceive people.
Empirical Evidence: Information acquired by observation or experimentation.
Enlightenment: A European intellectual movement of the late 17th and 18th centuries emphasizing reason and individualism rather than tradition.
Epistemology: The branch of philosophy that deals with the theory and nature of knowledge.
Evidence: Information or data used to support a claim or argument.
Fake News: False or misleading information presented as news.
Falsifiability: The ability of a theory or hypothesis to be proven wrong.
Generalization: A broad statement derived from specific instances.

Good Science: Scientific research that follows strict methodologies and ethical standards, subject to peer review.
Humanism: Emphasizing the potential value and goodness of human beings, common human needs, and seeking solely rational ways of solving human problems.
Hypothesis: A proposed explanation for a phenomenon that can be tested through experimentation or observation.
Inflation Theory: A theory of exponential expansion of space in the very early universe.
Internet: The global system of interconnected computer networks.
Intuition: Understanding something immediately, without the need for conscious reasoning.
Justification: The action of showing something to be right or reasonable.
Knowledge: Facts, information, and skills acquired through experience or education.
Logical Fallacy: An error in reasoning that renders an argument logically invalid.
Misinformation: False or inaccurate information spread regardless of intent.
Objective: Not influenced by personal feelings or opinions in considering and representing facts.
Peer Review: The evaluation of scientific or academic work by others working in the same field.
Probability: The likelihood of something happening or being the case.
Pseudoscience: Claims, beliefs, or practices presented as scientific but lacking the evidence or methodological rigor required of true science.
Rationalization: A defense mechanism in which controversial behaviors or feelings are justified and explained in a seemingly logical manner to avoid

the true explanation.
Reasoning: The action of thinking about something in a logical, sensible way.
Scientific Method: A systematic approach used in scientific research that involves observation, experimentation, and hypothesis testing.
Scientific Revolution: A period in European history, primarily during the 16th and 17th centuries, where significant advancements in science and mathematics dramatically changed our understanding of the natural world, marked by a shift from relying on ancient Greek thought to a more experimental and observation-based approach, leading to the foundation of modern science as we know it today; key figures include Copernicus, Galileo, Kepler, and Newton.
Skepticism: The attitude of doubting the truth of something, often applied to beliefs that lack sufficient evidence.
Social Brain Hypothesis: The idea that human intelligence evolved primarily as a means of surviving and reproducing in complex social groups.
Tenet: A principle or belief, especially one of the main principles of a religion or philosophy.
Tenets of Critical Thinking: Fundamental principles guiding effective reasoning and judgment.
Testability: The capacity of a hypothesis or theory to be proven false through experimentation.
Theory: A well-substantiated explanation of an aspect of the natural world, based on a body of evidence.
Unfalsifiable Claim: A statement or hypothesis that cannot be proven false, making it scientifically invalid.
Universe: The part of spacetime that was created by the Big Bang.

Validity: The quality of being logically or factually sound.
Vernal Equinox: The equinox in March, when the Sun crosses the celestial equator in a northerly direction, marking the beginning of Spring in the Northern Hemisphere.
Warrant: The justification for the connection between the evidence and the claim in an argument.

Index

A

Ad Hominem Fallacy, 109
Age of IoT (Internet of Things), 1
Age of Surveillance, 1
Alhazen, 10
Appeal to Authority Fallacy, 112-114
Appeal to Public Opinion Fallacy, 113
Appendix: Logical Fallacies, 105-122
Artificial Intelligence (AI), 5, 41, 89, 93-94, 123, 124
Assumption, Evidence, Conclusion, 19-21
Astrology, 62, 82, 123
Axioms of Science, 29-34, 64, 91-92, 123

C

Cause and Effect Fallacies, 119-122
Causes and Effects (Types of), 23-27, 91
Circular Reasoning Fallacy, 107-108
Cognitive Bias, 48, 78, 112, 122, 123
Correlation Does Not Imply Causation, 23, 31

Critical Thinking, 2, 5-6, 9-17, 29, 35, 68, 81, 83, 91, 93, 94, 124
Cum Hoc Ergo Propter Hoc Fallacy, 120

D

Debunking, 5, 81-90, 91, 92, 124
Deep Fakes, 2, 5, 81-90, 94, 124
Differentiating Between Good Science, Outdated Science, and Pseudoscience, 51-56, 91-92
Disinformation, 2-3, 5, 75, 81-90, 93-94, 124
Distinction Without a Difference Fallacy, 106

E

Empiricism, 30, 40, 53, 67, 71, 124
Enlightenment, 69, 124
Epistemology, 67-72, 124
Equivocation Fallacy, 105
Extra Sensory Perception (ESP), 82

F

Faith Healing, 63, 82
Fake News, 2, 5, 89-90, 94, 124
Fallacy of Affirming the Consequent, 120-121

Fallacy of Composition, 114, 115
Fallacy of the Continuum, 114, 116-117
Fallacy of Denying the Antecedent, 119,121
Fallacy of Division, 114-116
Fallacy of False Alternatives, 114-115
Fallacy of the Golden Mean, 114, 115
Fallacy of Negative Proof, 108-109
Fallacy of Tradition, 114
Flawed Assumption Fallacies, 64, 114
Faulty Analogy Fallacy, 114, 118
Francis Bacon, 10, 95

G
Gambler's Fallacy, 114, 119
Geocentric Universe, 53
Germ Theory of Disease, 33, 51
Golden Age of Islam, 10
Good Current Science, 51-52, 91, 92, 98

H
H. pylori, 43, 113
Hasty Generalization Fallacy, 21, 106-107
Hypothesis, 10-11, 124, 125, 126

I
Image Reverse Search, 90
Incorrect Attack on a Generalization Fallacy, 114, 117
Information Age, 1-2, 94
Internet, 1-3, 86, 88, 93, 125
Irrelevancies Fallacy, 110-112

J
JFK Assassination Conspiracy, 60-61

L
Logical Fallacies, 19-21, 31, 64, 82, 83, 91, 105-122, 125

M
Magical Thinking, 24, 91
Misinformation, 2-7, 81-90, 91, 93, 94, 123, 125

N
Natural Causes for Events, 29-30, 96
Necessary Cause, 25-26
Non-Sequitur Fallacy, 31, 110-111

O

Observation, 10-11, 30-31, 35-36, 37, 124, 125, 126
Outdated Science, 52-54, 91, 92, 98

P

Peer Review, 35, 38, 84, 125
Poisoning the Well Fallacy, 109-110
Post Hoc Ergo Propter Hoc Fallacy, 119-120
Prediction, 36-38, 40, 97-98
Principles of Logic, 19-21, 91
Pseudoscience, 54-56, 57, 62, 63, 83, 84, 91-92, 125
Purposes of reasoning, 14-15

R

Rationality, 64, 70, 92, 125
Reason/Reasoning, vii, 4, 12, 13-17, 29, 68, 83, 91, 96, 107, 123-126

S

Scientific Method, 10-11, 29, 35-49, 67, 68, 91-92, 96, 98, 126
Scientific Revolution, 53, 69, 126
Single Cause, Multiple Effects, 26

Skepticism, 35, 85-86, 126
Slippery Slope Fallacy, 114, 118
Social Brain Hypothesis, 14-15, 126
Straw Man, 114, 117-118
Sufficient Cause, 25

T

Tautology, 107-108
Temporal Precedence, 23
Tenets of Critical Thinking, 95-99, 126
Tu Quoque Fallacy, 109, 110
Types of Reasoning, 14-15, 91

V

Vaccines and Autism, 55-56

W

Wishful Thinking Fallacy (cognitive bias), 110, 112
Wizardry and Witchcraft, 63

www.ingramcontent.com/pod-product-compliance
Lightning Source LLC
Chambersburg PA
CBHW070633030426
42337CB00020B/3996